This book is dedicated to Mother Nature

 za

Contents

Preface

The need for the new revised edition of this book is due to the continuing demand for knowledge and skills related to backpacking. Within these pages can be found the most contemporary information available on the subject today, including the latest details on backpacking equipment, hiking fundamentals, and even off-trail travel techniques.

The book is appropriately used either as a self-study source for those who want to learn the skills of hiking and camping, or as a text for courses in outdoor education, physical education, environmental education, outdoor leadership, or any other learning situation where the skills of backpacking might be taught. It also provides a pertinent reference for those who are already involved or experienced in the ways of backcountry travel. The ultimate goal of the author is to develop sophisticated hikers who are capable of going anywhere for any reasonable length of time, with the confidence to safely enjoy the experience.

The emphasis in the following pages is on traveling simply and lightly. Also, there is a strong orientation to what is known as the wilderness ethic—understanding and appreciating the natural environment and reducing human impact on the land. The text provides basic knowledge and understanding of *why* we should be concerned with our impact on the environment and *how* we can enjoy the backcountry without spoiling it. Employing a scientific rationale, the text discusses the most recent knowledge of backpacking in an easy-to-read, straightforward manner.

Although it is not possible to list all of those who provided encouragement and assistance throughout the development of the concepts and materials for the second edition of this book, I would like to thank all of my former students who have shared their thoughts around many campfires. At the same time, I also wish to express my appreciation and deep respect to Cal Tassinari, recently retired U.S. Forest Service Wilderness Ranger. During the past two decades, Cal has unselfishly permitted me to share his great wisdom and knowledge of the Montana wilderness.

1

WHY BACKPACK AND WHERE TO GO

Why Backpack?

As our society has changed over the years, and as we have grown away from our ancestors' close reliance on, and affiliation with nature, so too have we found a need to reacquaint ourselves with that real world. As more of us move into larger cities and suburbs, we discover a loss of something that almost borders on the spiritual. Some would say we need to "get away from it all," while others prefer to think of it as a need for personal involvement, enrichment, and renewal.

Backpacking surely stands out as a means of reestablishing our roots, of bringing us into harmony with our heritage of the outdoors, and for giving a perspective beyond that obtained in the narrow confines of a crowded society. Also, this form of activity can help in the development of other desirable physical, mental, social, and spiritual qualities. For example, studies have indicated that participation in outdoor challenge activities, such as backpacking, often can lead to positive measurable effects in elements of self-concept (including self-reliance and self-confidence), development of environmental awareness, aesthetic appreciation, cooperation, physical fitness, ability to deal with stress, and tenacity (1,2,3,4,5).

Perhaps the essence of backpacking as a form of recreation is in the individual freedom it allows: freedom to be independent from the use of modern society's gadgetry and a contrast in the form of a chance for solitude, in which individuals can achieve freedom from their own problems. At the same time, it also presents the opportunity for enjoying companionship with others, sharing joys and hardships, learning the meaning of humility, and developing open dialogue among peers. Of course, much of the appeal of backpacking is embodied in the enjoyment of scenery that can't be viewed from a car, and the physical challenge of doing something on one's own that demands hard work.

In addition, backpacking leads to some of the best opportunities to enjoy fishing, hunting, wildlife photography, nature study, and other forms of outdoor recreation. Wilderness and other unroaded areas inaccessible by motorized vehicles are usually ideal locations for these activities.

Learning can be enhanced in the outdoors, and consequently backpacking is a good tool for learning about yourself and others. Education should be regarded as the sum total of life experiences, whether in the home, school, work, or recreation environment. In this respect, backpacking is unique in that it is a total experience in itself, a twenty-four-hour-a-day adventure outdoors. Here, in an intensely personal way, is provided a chance to expand our understanding and appreciation for others because we are living and working together in a small group where there are many opportunities for assuming a share of the work, for give-and-take, for group decision making, and for building closer friendships. Also, individual growth and development comes about through opportunities to discover one's own potential and to exercise personal initiative.

The increased emphasis on the understanding and wise use of the environment has also become an important aspect of backpacking. Regard for the environment can result in better care of our immediate surroundings, as well as a better feeling about our place in the universe and the resources upon which the quality of life depends. Outdoor-related skills and knowledge, including care of the environment, will have increasing importance as a greater number of people seek a natural experience in their leisure.

Certainly we cannot overlook the enjoyment and satisfaction that comes from engaging in an adventurous and challenging outing experience. Backpacking, as a form of outdoor recreation, is an end in itself and, as such, needs no further justification beyond the satisfaction it provides the participant. This activity is enhanced by the fact that it can be engaged in by people of all age groups throughout life. It also can be pursued almost anywhere in the world, either singly or with small groups of friends.

These are some of the reasons that large numbers of people are turning to backpacking as a popular form of outdoor recreation; hiking and backpacking provide a wonderful opportunity for a real change of pace, a chance to get away from it all, and to get back to nature and rediscover those things that have true meaning in life. The newfound awareness of this activity must also be attributed, in part, to longer vacation periods, more spendable income, and the development of more functional recreational equipment. Whatever the reason, backpacking continues to maintain its popularity.

For these reasons, it is little wonder that steadily increasing numbers of people are fleeing the cities to pursue their recreational desires in backcountry and wilderness areas. Today there are millions of backpackers in America, with the numbers growing steadily each year. Walking for pleasure and the use of the wilderness have been expanding at faster rates than most other forms of outdoor recreation, and this growth extends to all age groups, including many families.

Where to Backpack

To the backpacker, places to hike are as vital as wilderness is to the grizzly bear or free-flowing streams are to the Atlantic salmon. Despite what you may think, however, there is no shortage of places to go hiking or camping. In the high country resplendent in scenic beauty, hikers encounter alpine forests, glacier ice fields, and lava flows, as well as deserts, tundra, wildlife, and trout streams galore. Also available for our pleasure at lower elevations are river bottoms, rolling prairies, hardwood forests, lowland marshes, and the edges of the seas. In many places you are exhilarated by the grandeur of nature, and enveloped in the same solitude of open spaces experienced by the pioneers.

Nor does one need to travel long distances from home to find suitable areas for backpacking; some very outstanding hiking country exists close to urban environments. Probably 10 to 15 percent of all hiking takes place in established wilderness, while another 10 to 15 percent is on national forest trails outside wilderness areas. This means that approximately two-thirds of all hiking is done on state, county, and private lands.

Trail Systems

To meet the ever-increasing outdoor recreation needs of an expanding population, and to provide access to, travel within, and enjoyment and appreciation of the outdoors, trails are being established by federal, state, and local governments. The United States has nearly 200,000 miles of existing trails. There are also private trail systems that cater to public needs, and there are many unofficial, unmaintained paths around cities and towns.

In 1968, Congress adopted a significant law benefiting backpackers—the National Trails System Act. This established a system of scenic and recreational trails in order to provide hikers relief from concrete and motorized traffic.

Originally, two National Scenic Trails were designated by the law—the Appalachian Trail and the Pacific Crest Trail—and since then, six other trails have been added. Together they encompass more than 14,000 miles in 32 states and the District of Columbia. Side and connecting trails also provide access to and between various components of each of these trails, making it possible to hike various segments without completing the entire route. A listing of the eight existing National Scenic Trails and the lengths of their Congressionally-established routes can be found in Appendix A.

America's classic long-distance trails are perhaps best represented by the Appalachian, Pacific Crest, and Continental Divide National Scenic Trails. The 2,146-mile Appalachian Trail extends generally along the Appalachian Mountains from Springer Mountain in Georgia to Mount Katahdin, Maine. It is accessible to people living in the metropolitan centers along the Atlantic seaboard. The trail and surrounding lands are maintained and managed by the non-profit Appalachian Trail Conference (P.O. Box 807, Harpers Ferry, WV 25425), and volunteers in

31 of its clubs, under special agreement with the National Park Service, U.S. Forest Service, and state governments.

At the other end of the country, the Pacific Crest Trail runs approximately 2,638 miles and extends from the Mexico-California border northward, generally along the mountain ranges of the west coast states to the Canada-Washington border near Lake Ross. The trail follows the ridges of the Cascades and the Sierra Nevadas, amid spectacular mountain formations and awesome vistas. The portion of the trail in Washington is known as the Cascade Crest Trail. In Oregon it is known as the Oregon Skyline Trail. The several segments in California are known as the Lava Crest Trail, the Tahoe-Yosemite Trail, the John Muir Trail, the Sierra Trail, and the Desert Crest Trail. The Forest Service, Park Service, and Bureau of Land Management, with the help of volunteers, maintain the stretches of the Pacific Crest Trail across their lands. More than 2,000 miles of the route are on Forest Service land, making it the principal management agency for the trail. For further details, contact the Pacific Crest Trail Coordinator at either the U.S. Forest Service Pacific Northwest Regional Office, or the Pacific Southwest Regional Office. Addresses can be found in Appendix B.

The Continental Divide National Scenic Trail is considered the most rugged of all America's trails and was added to the National Trails System in 1978. It provides a spectacular backcountry experience for 3,200 miles along the crest of the Rocky Mountains running from the Canadian border to Mexico. Beginning in Glacier National Park, Montana, the trail traverses such fabulous wild country as the Bob Marshall Wilderness, the Anaconda-Pintler Wilderness, Yellowstone National Park, Rocky Mountain National Park, and the Gila Wilderness. Further information on this trail can be obtained by contacting the Continental Divide Trail Society (P.O. Box 30002, Bethesda, MD 20814) or the U.S. Forest Service Continental Divide Trail Coordinator Offices in the Northern Region, Rocky Mountain Region, and Southwestern Region. Addresses are listed in Appendix B.

Other National Scenic Trail routes include the following:

1) The Potomac Heritage Trail, which follows the banks of the history-rich Potomac River for 700 miles through Pennsylvania, West Virginia, Maryland, Washington, D.C., and Virginia;

2) The Natchez Trail, a 600-mile route first used by Indians, then traders, later becoming the early-day path between Nashville, Tennessee, and Natchez, on the lower Mississippi River;

(3) The North Country Trail, which covers 3,200 miles through New York, Pennsylvania, Ohio, Michigan, Wisconsin, Minnesota, and North Dakota;

4) The Ice Age National Scenic Trail, which follows a thousand-mile-long ridge of hills in Wisconsin created thousands of years ago by the retreating glaciers of the Ice Age; and

5) The 1,300-mile-long Florida Trail linking the western end of the Florida panhandle to Lake Okeechobee, and then continuing on to the Big Cypress National Preserve.

At the time the National Trails System Act was initiated, forty more trails were named as National Recreation Trails to be administered by local, state, or federal agencies, while a number of other trails were identified for study as possible future additions. Today more than 780 National Recreation Trails, ranging in length from a fraction of a mile to almost 500 miles, have become a part of the National Trails System.

Before leaving this discussion, it should be mentioned that an additional trail category, namely National Historic Trails, was added to the National Trails System in 1978. The intent of this designation was to recognize past routes of exploration, migration, and military action. The nine existing National Historic Trails approved for inclusion in this category are listed in Appendix A. Further information on these trails can be obtained by contacting the National Trails System Branch, Recreation Resources Assistance Division, National Park Service, Washington, D.C.

Wilderness

Perhaps the most significant event to benefit avid backpackers took place when Congress passed the Wilderness Act in 1964, initially setting aside a little more than nine million acres of land in 60 areas under protection as a part of the National Wilderness Preservation System. These lands, and others that have more recently been classified as "wilderness," are administered for the use and enjoyment of the American people. Areas qualified as wilderness must be undeveloped federal land retaining its primeval character, and must provide outstanding opportunities for solitude as a primitive and unconfined type of recreation.

In 1975, the Eastern Wilderness Act identified a need to add additional areas to the Wilderness System, primarily in the East. Some areas were designated immediately and others were identified for wilderness study. Since then, other areas throughout the United States have also been brought under protection, and yet additional areas are now under study and may be recommended to Congress as wilderness.

Today, the National Wilderness Preservation System contains over 90 million acres of designated wilderness at 474 locations in 43 different states. These areas are found in national forests, national parks, national wildlife refuges, and on public land administered by the Bureau of Land Management. The chart in Appendix C identifies the number of wilderness area units and acres of wilderness found in each state. Appendix C also reveals that the majority of wilderness units are managed by the U.S. Forest Service, while the National Park Service manages a large amount of overall wilderness acreage.

State and local governments also have set aside areas of land to be preserved in their natural state and managed as wilderness. Several states have established wilderness systems within their boundaries, while a number of others have established legislation or have already designated areas that preserve land in a natural condition.

Forests and Grasslands

National forests and national grasslands are located in 41 states—extending from the Atlantic Coast in the Carolinas, to the redwoods and sand dunes along the Pacific beaches. Swamps along the Gulf of Mexico, the high plains of North America, and deserts of the Southwest are all found within the National Forests and Grasslands system, administered by the U.S. Forest Service. Today, nearly 60 million acres of these lands remain roadless and undeveloped—some 2,000 areas in every region of the country. These remarkable areas are called "de facto wilderness," because they have no formal designation or protection as wilderness. Even so, these lands provide an opportunity for all people to use and enjoy them.

Public Domain

The Bureau of Land Management (BLM) is our nation's largest land custodian, overseeing 272 million acres of beautiful frontier land. These public lands range from saguaro-cactus desert to Douglas-fir forest, and from rolling range land to Arctic tundra. Overall, they comprise about 46 percent of the federally-owned lands in the United States, or about one-eighth of our nation's total land area. These lands are located primarily in 11 Western states.

Since the BLM was not even mentioned in the Wilderness Act of 1964, the Bureau administratively developed its own primitive and natural areas system. Between 1969 and 1976, it set aside 55 different primitive or natural areas–a total of 505,000 acres. However, legislation passed in 1976 provided a mandate for the BLM to review its roadless wildlands for their potential for inclusion in the Wilderness Preservation System. While only 25 wilderness units, or slightly more than 450,000 acres, have now been approved for inclusion, there are an additional 855 wilderness study areas, covering 25 million acres, undergoing assessment to determine their suitability for inclusion in the National Wilderness Preservation System.

Other Areas

The National Park Service administers millions of acres of park lands, commonly referred to as the "crown jewels" of the country. As already mentioned, and as is revealed in Appendix C, many of our national park lands are part of the National Wilderness Preservation System. Also, the U.S. Fish and Wildlife Service administers 376 units of the National Wildlife System for the perpetuation of wildlife and their habitats. Much of this land, which is ideal for hiking and camping purposes, falls under wilderness classification.

We would be remiss to overlook such fine backpacking resources as those provided by most of our state park systems throughout the United States. Although most are smaller in size and grandeur than many of the federal parks and wildernesses, their ready access and suitability cannot be down-played. Adirondack Park in New York is a splendid example of a true wilderness park in a populated state.

General recreation maps and related information about most of the areas mentioned in this chapter are available from the appropriate land-managing agency. Names and addresses of some of these agencies can be found in Appendix B.

As can be seen, there is plenty of elbow room out there in what might best be referred to as "backcountry," so let's next discuss the equipment and skills used to get us there.

1. Breitenstein, Donna, and Alan Ewert. 1990. "Health Benefits of Outdoor Recreation: Implications for Health Education," *Health Education* vol. 21, no. 1, Jan./Feb. pp. 16-20.

2. Bunting, Camille J. 1989. "Experiences in the Wilderness: Opportunities for Health," *Trends*, vol. 26, no. 3, pp. 9-13.

3. Ewert, Alan W. 1989. *Outdoor Adventure Pursuits: Foundations, Models, and Theories.* Publishing Horizons, Inc., 234 pp.

4. Ewert, Alan. n.d. *Outdoor Adventure and Self-Concept: A Research Analysis.* Center for Leisure Studies, Department of Recreation and Park Management, University of Oregon, Eugene, 36 pp.

5. Miles, John. 1987. "Wilderness as Healing Place," *Journal of Experiential Education*, vol. 10, no. 3, pp. 4-10.

2

EQUIPMENT AND CLOTHING

In order to maintain a healthy existence in the outdoors, we require three essentials—food (including water), shelter, and insulation. Of course, a backpack is also needed to carry all of these things. Unfortunately, we also desire to maintain a sense of comfort beyond what is provided by those ingredients alone. Thus, we are faced with the dilemma of choosing what to take along. Ideally we could provide both required and desired items, and still be able to carry our weighted pack, but this is most likely not the case. Far too many inexperienced groups coming into the backcountry are so over-equipped with heavy, unnecessary items that they find only hard work, instead of a pleasant outing. Somehow, by keeping our requirements few and simple, we must decide on the most desired items and leave the rest at home. This means squeezing the most use out of the least equipment. How to do this, and what to take along are discussed in this chapter.

Appendix D presents a checklist of common items that might be needed on a backcountry excursion (also see Fig. 2.1). Compare your needs with this list and then prepare a personal check sheet of items based on your particular needs. Remember that equipment and clothing requirements will vary depending on a number of factors, such as length of trip, time of year, and location of travel. Keep your check sheet in a convenient location for handy reference each time you prepare for an outing. Through trial and error, the list can be revised or updated following each excursion.

Fig. 2.1. All essentials needed for a backpack trip. First row: backpack and sleeping bag, groundcloth, tent, pad, clothing, parka. Second row: Rain pants, boots, camp shoes, socks, towel, down sweater in stuff sack. Third row: stove, fuel container with pump, pot, water bottle, cup, spoon, pocket knife, matches in waterproof container, flashlight, toilet paper and lighter, small bag with liquid soap, dental floss, toothbrush, toothpaste, water filter. Fourth row: sunglasses, first aid kit, whistle, bug lotion, candle, compass, map, camera, nylon cord, food supplies in bag.

Backpacks

Modern backpacks are partially responsible for the increased popularity of hiking and camping in the wilderness. There are many different models from which to choose, so you should know what to look for in terms of materials and workmanship. A good pack should become an old friend, as it will last a long time. A poor selection here could mean serious trouble for you if problems arise with your pack while deep in the backcountry. No one needs the aggravation of a broken shoulder strap or snapped frame, let alone a strained muscle or well-worn blister from a poor fit.

Types of Packs

Packs are often classified by size. The *expedition pack* is the largest and is used for carrying loads on extended trips of several days or more. At midsize is the *overnight pack,* which is big enough for limited food and clothing as well as a sleeping bag. *Day packs* are the smallest of the choices, and their limited volume makes them impractical for overnight use. This small pack is frequently used for carrying a lunch and other accessories while on short side trips away from a base camp.

In addition to size, backpacks can be grouped by their type of suspension system. For instance, one type is the *frameless pack,* which has been around for as long as anyone can remember. Due to the nature of these rucksacks, they enforce the discipline of packing light and leaving extraneous items behind. Their primary disadvantage for backpacking is that most of the weight in the pack is born on your shoulders. This, then, forces the center of gravity away from your body unless compensated by a forward lean. The softness of the bag also creates a problem in loading, because heavy items placed toward the top often cause the pack to sag.

Internal frame packs have a rigid frame system built into the pack bag, so they are sturdier, and spread the weight more evenly on the back, thus eliminating many of the shortcomings of the frameless models (see Fig. 2.2). Also, the internal frame pack allows you plenty of freedom of motion by snugging the load close to your back with a flexible, form-fitting frame. Both the frameless and internal frame packs are popular among mountain climbers and cross-country skiers, because they fit snugly on the back and do not hinder elbow and arm movements along the side of the body. The internal frame pack is also very suitable for backpacking, but it is especially ideal for scrambling and off-trail travel through rough terrain.

The *external frame pack* is most commonly used for carrying heavy loads on extended backpacking trips, especially when traveling on decent trails and moderately rough terrain. As the name suggests, this pack has its frame or support system outside the packbag. The packbag attaches to the back of an exposed rigid frame made of aluminum tubing, molded-nylon, or plastic. The shoulder straps as well as a backband and hip belt attach to the front of the frame. The advantage of the rigid frame is that much of the weight normally placed on the shoulders is transferred to the back, hips, and legs. This allows the load to ride high and more in line with your vertical walking axis. Thus, the carry is more comfortable because you are allowed to stand straight. Also, since the structure of an external frame pack holds the packbag away from your back, plenty of cool-air can circulate between the pack and your back.

Fig. 2.2. Rigid expedition packs. Left: the internal frame pack. Right: the external frame pack.

Pack Selection

In addition to deciding on style, there are a number of other things to consider when selecting a backpack. For instance, the pack frame can be one of several shapes, including the conventional *straight ladder* and *S ladder designs*. The S ladder frame is contoured to fit the arch of your back and is usually more comfortable than the straight ladder design. Recent experiments have also resulted in contemporary frame designs referred to as *hip wrap* and *figure eight models*. Some of these are made of flexible materials that permit the upper and lower sections of the frame to flex in separate directions from one another as do the hiker's shoulders and thighs when walking.

Frame construction must be sturdy to withstand hard use. Inspect the joints of cross bars on a frame made of aluminum tubing. These joints should be solidly welded or bolted together. Also, some frames are adjustable to different sizes for an accurate fit. This is a real advantage if the pack is to be used by several different persons. Some models even provide a pull-out extension at the top of the frame for additional load capacity if needed.

Make sure your pack's shoulder straps are adequately padded to ease the discomfort of heavy loads. Straps should be adjustable for length and shoulder width. The waist belt should also be padded and, for safety purposes, should have a quick-release buckling system so the pack can be jettisoned. To keep the pack from rubbing on your back, a nylon mesh back band should be provided. The mesh also allows your back to stay dry, because perspiration does not accumulate or soak in (see Fig. 2.3).

Fig. 2.3. The backpack should be both sturdy and comfortable. Ample padding is needed in the waist belt and shoulder straps. A nylon mesh back band is also important.

The packbag itself, as well as the strap attachments, should have good reinforcing and extra stitching at stress points. Make sure the stitching is not too close to the edge of the seam or the edge of the material, as this can cause it to come apart. An adequate number of external pockets, including one for a map, should be sewn on the sides and top of the pack. Pockets and openings should have heavy-duty zippers. Further, some bags are designed to be loaded from the top, and others have separate horizontal compartments. The difference here is a matter of personal choice.

With respect to capacity, the average packbag suitable for most one- to three-night trips is between 3,000 and 3,300 cubic inches on an external frame. Keep in mind that the bottom portion of an external frame pack is clear to accommodate a sleeping bag. In contrast, an internal frame pack used to carry approximately the same amount of equipment needs to be at least 4,000 cubic inches, because the sleeping bag goes inside the packbag. For additional information on backpacks, including determination of carrying weight, how to wear the pack, and techniques for packing, see Chapter 5.

Tents and Shelters

There is nothing so pleasurable as sleeping in the open with the stars for a roof. Even so, any time you plan to stay overnight away from civilization, serious consideration must be given to the potential need for shelter. On occasion, shielding yourself from the elements (wind, rain, cold, snow, or even mosquitos) may be more than a matter of comfort and convenience; it could be a matter of survival. Many persons are unaware, for instance, that most cases of hypothermia occur when the temperature is well above the freezing mark. Even during the warmest season in the driest of climates, you are never assured that unusual weather will not occur.

A variety of shelter options can be considered, depending on the time of year and where you want to go. At times, a tarp or canopy might serve you well, while on other occasions, a tent is definitely in order. Learn the weather patterns in the area you plan to visit before deciding. Also, be sure to consider your normal usage requirements rather than what might be needed for that once-in-a-lifetime expedition. Generally, the tent can provide the best assurance of protection for a few additional pounds in your pack; but in good weather, money and weight can be saved with a simple shelter from a poncho or tarp. It is important, however, to realize their limitations.

Canopies Other Than Tents

Although you are confined to a very small space, a *poncho* can provide adequate protection from rain if erected in a very low profile. Be sure to get one with tabs or grommets suitable for tying on lines. Also, because there may not be nearby trees or bushes to lash onto, consider bringing poles and pegs.

Another inexpensive means of providing shelter is to use *polyethylene* or *plastic sheets*, which are available in various thicknesses and sizes. For adequate strength, nothing less than two mil thickness should be considered. A sheet measuring 9 x 12 feet is quite light, yet is suitable for constructing various shelter designs. With ingenuity, many different kinds of shelters can be created. One common way of setting up a shelter is to establish a ridge line between two trees or poles and then pitch the plastic material over the line in "pup tent" fashion. The edges can be weighted down with rocks or by tying on cords and connecting to stakes. Plastic stick-on grommets can be taped onto the sheet for tie cords. Another method of attachment is to fold each edge of the tarp around a small stone and then tie off the stone with cord, which is then attached to stakes. In place of stones, a handful of grass can be used. Simply wad up the grass and tie it off in the same way. The rock or clump of grass allows a firm grasp for the cord, which otherwise would tear loose from the plastic sheet.

In addition to serving as a shelter, polyethylene can be used for a number of other things, such as a groundcloth, tablecloth, or water bag. The longevity or usefulness of the material is usually limited to several trips because it can puncture or tear easily. Should it become unusable because of damage, be sure to pack it out of the backcountry.

The single layer tarp made of waterproof coated nylon can provide flexible and durable protection against the elements. Tarps are available in various sizes, and come with grommets around the edges. Some also have tie tabs conveniently spaced in the middle, for suspension of the sheet from a tree branch or ridge line. A nylon tarp measuring 9 x 10 feet is light, and allows plenty of sleeping room for two persons plus gear. As with the poncho and plastic sheet, the nylon fly should be erected with a low profile in order to shed wind and rain (see Fig. 2.4). One method is to arrange the fly with one ridge almost touching the ground and the other suspended only three or four feet higher. The sides can be pulled down as far as desired as long as adequate room remains inside for the inhabitants.

Fig. 2.4. A tarp erected in low profile provides protection against the elements.

Tents

The general quality of backpacking tents has greatly improved in recent years. Manufacturing technology has advanced at such a rapid rate that there is an ever-increasing assortment of fabrics, sizes, and designs from which to choose. Considerations in selecting a tent include the following factors.

Dryness. The tent should keep out rain and moisture. A waterproof "bathtub" style floor, extending up the side walls several inches, will protect gear from ground moisture.

Insect Protection. Netting and closures in doors and vents will provide an insect-free place to sleep while allowing ventilation. Air circulation is important to help evaporate condensation in the tent created by body moisture.

Rain Fly. A single-wall, waterproof nylon tent will shed rain, but because of the cooler temperatures outside the tent, body moisture condenses on the inside of the tent. The best-known method of reducing condensation inside a tent is to rely on a two-layered ceiling. This is called double-wall construction. The inner ceiling of the tent is made of untreated cloth to provide maximum breathability, which allows water vapor to pass through it. A separate plastic-coated nylon fly is placed over the inner ceiling, but is separated from it by a few inches. This fly sheds rain, yet allows the inner tent to remain well-ventilated and dry. Water vapor passing through the inner wall will condense on the underside of the fly. Also, a rain fly will keep a tent considerably cooler in the summer, and warmer in the winter, because of the added shade and insulation factor.

Bulk and Weight. No matter how innovative its design, a backpacking tent must be lightweight and compact. On an average, the tent should weigh around three pounds per person. The more people the tent is designed for, the less it should weigh per person.

Space. A tent must provide a functional amount of living space for its particular use. The intended purpose of the tent should dictate not only its design, but also the amount of needed space. For example, a summer ultralight tent primarily used for backpacking would have very little space except for sleeping. On the other hand, an expedition-type tent might be heavier but more roomy, because it is also frequently used for other things, such as cooking and storage. Also, you must consider whether the tent will be used by only one or two people, or whether three or more will call it home. There is little sense in carrying a large tent that is used by only two people.

Design. Tent manufacturers are developing some interesting new designs in shapes and frame systems. Modified tepees, free-standing box tents, and dome tents have become popular because they offer more room inside and can be erected easily. Tunnel designs have also grown in popularity. Recent advances in flexible fiberglass and aluminum pole materials have revolutionized the entire market.

Dome and tunnel tents have greater space—nearly 50 percent more volume than A-frame tents with the same floor area.

Because of their vertical side walls, they are more comfortable to live in when the occupants become stormbound. In spite of all this, some of the traditional A-frame models are still lighter and more secure than many of the new designs.

Tent shape is best thought of in terms of the floor plan, which is generally oval or rectangular. The important thing is not square-footage numbers, but how the floor plan is used. The rectangle is most efficient at holding the human body, while an oval tent of the same square footage holds fewer people, but allows more gear storage.

Keep in mind that different tent designs are affected by wind, rain, and snow in different ways. Low-profile tents of the A-frame design are generally the most practical in areas of heavy wind because the design presents a relatively small surface area. If pitched with one end facing a gale, the A-frame tent is very stable. In contrast, a free-standing dome tent usually relies on the flexibility of the pole system to accommodate the wind. Keep in mind that wind gusts of over 50 miles per hour are not uncommon above mountain timberline or on exposed ridges. Damage can be caused from such extraordinary stress on the curved, springy pole joints.

Material and Construction. A tent is only as good as its material, the primary ingredient being the fabric. Before World War II, tents were usually made of heavy canvas. However, canvas and other cotton fabrics used in tents presented many problems, such as mildew and weight. In contrast, a nylon tent is much lighter and stronger. Nylon remains the most common fabric used in modern backpacking tents, but newer, complex, and expensive materials, such as Gore-Tex laminates, are on the rise (the name Gore-Tex is a registered trademark).

Gore-Tex is a unique water-repellent material, which, due to its small pores, also breathes. Water vapor molecules are allowed to pass through it, but larger water droplets cannot. As a result, when using Gore-Tex fabric in tents, the need for a fly is supposedly reduced or eliminated.

Nylon fabric comes in two different weaves. One is taffeta, a flat weave fabric with smooth, unbroken texture. The other is rip-stop nylon, which has a weave with two threads twisted together in a rectangular pattern spaced at about quarter-inch intervals.

This reinforcing helps to stop tears and to distribute stress over a greater area. Rip-stop nylon is lighter in weight than taffeta, and is less likely to tear. If nylon fabric is to be waterproof, it must be coated with urethane. Nontreated nylon is used for tent canopies and inner ceilings, as it is breathable.

Most good tents should have well-designed poles that are shock-corded—poles that are strung together by elastic cords running through the hollow tubes. Poles that do not have this feature take longer to assemble, and can fall apart while being threaded through pole sleeves; also, individual sections can be easily lost. Shock-corded poles eliminate the problem of matching up the right sections— a very difficult task if you are assembling the tent in the dark.

Other factors to look for in tent materials and construction are strong zippers, good stitching, and desired extra accessories. A sturdy tent will have heavy-duty zippers with pull-tabs on both sides, so they can be closed whether you are inside or out. Nylon zippers are considered stronger than metal ones, which tend to freeze. The tent itself should be well made with strong, double-stitched "lapped" seams and sturdy grommets. Accessories might include inside pockets for storage of small items, a vestibule for larger things, a zipper hole in the floor of the tent for cooking in bad weather, snow flaps for anchoring the tent in the winter, and a frostliner, which stops frost buildup on tent walls when temperatures dip below freezing.

A final, but most important consideration in selecting a tent, is that of correctly matching the shelter to the climatic conditions for which it will be used. Fortunately for the consumer, most tent manufacturers categorize their tents according to intended seasonal use. The major determinants are generally construction characteristics and weatherproofing features. The common tent classifications used include (1) summer/screen tents, (2) three-season tents, and (3) four-season tents. *Summer/Screen Tents* usually consist of a net canopy, a serviceable floor, and minimal rain protection. This combination maximizes ventilation and bug protection while reducing weight. Most backpacking shelters fall into the category of *Three-Season Tents*, which means they will handle anything but frigid, blustery winter weather. Most of these tents integrate a breathable inner canopy and a waterproof fly. *Four-Season Tents* are designed to keep you snug and dry in extremely nasty weather. Often a four-season tent is identical to the three-season version, except netting sidewalls have been replaced with nylon fabric to retain heat generated by warm bodies inside (see Fig. 2.5 a). Such a tent can keep the interior 10 to 20 degrees warmer than outside. Four-season tents also feature sturdier pole arrangements designed to bear or shed heavy snowfall, higher-sided "tub" floors to shrug off wind-driven precipitation, and extra lash tabs for guying the structure down in severe wind blasts.

Fig. 2.5 a. Four-season free-standing dome tent with rain fly removed.

Tent Care

Most tents are not factory seam-sealed. Consequently, the manufacturer will usually include a tube of seam-sealer, such as Aqua Seal, and instructions for application to the tent's fly and floor seams. Prior to taking the tent on its initial outing, be sure to apply the seam-seal carefully, for even a small leak in a seam can result in a rain-soaked sleeping bag. Seam-sealing can literally mean the difference between serious hypothermia and staying dry.

With proper care, a good tent should last over many years of rugged use. It is worthwhile to mention that you should be

Fig. 2.5 b. Three-season free-standing tunnel design with rain fly removed. Note large netted panels for excellent ventilation.

Fig. 2.5 c. Same tent, covered with rain fly and vestibule.

careful not to allow your tent to come in contact with sharp or abrasive surfaces. Be sure the campsite is reasonably clear of sharp sticks or rocks, and use a groundsheet to add an extra layer of protection for the bottom of the tent. A nylon tarp or sheet of heavy-duty poly plastic can serve as the groundsheet. Make sure the edges don't protrude or they will catch and puddle rainwater under the tent floor. Also, it is not desirable to store a wet tent for long periods of time, because zipper tabs and cotton stitching can rot, and mildew can penetrate the urethane coating of the fabric. Keep the tent clean by sweeping or sponging it before storage. If the fabric requires deeper cleaning, hand wash the tent with mild soap in lukewarm water.

See Chapter 5 for additional information on tent pitching.

Sleeping Bags

A sleeping bag is an important piece of outdoor equipment, because it directly relates to the amount of rest you get after a long day on the trail. As it is one of the more costly camping items, you would do well to shop around and choose carefully. There is a large assortment of selections on the market with a variety of qualities to consider. In order to know the alternatives, and to judge appropriately, it is important to become familiar with insulation properties as well as construction and design techniques.

Insulation

The purpose of insulation in a sleeping bag is to maintain a person's body temperature in a comfortable zone. To stay comfortable, we must be sure not to lose heat faster than it is produced. When the air is cold, heat is lost more easily. To decrease this heat loss, a layer of insulation is placed between the body surface and the cold air in order to create a space of dead air. It is primarily this space of dead air within the sleeping bag that keeps us warm.

In actuality, any material that creates a dead airspace will provide effective insulation; foam, polyester, down, or even newspapers will work. For the most part, the degree of warmth depends not on the type of material but on the thickness or "loft" of dead airspace it creates. The colder the temperature, the thicker the insulation needed. Also, the amount of insulation does not necessarily depend on how much material is used, or how much the sleeping bag weighs. For example, insulation is not improved by adding additional material to the same confined space once it is already filled enough to deaden the air. Therefore, you would get no more warmth out of 5 pounds of down in a sleeping bag than 1 pound in the same bag, unless the extra material gave the bag more loft.

Loft should be measured from your body outward, not from the ground up. As a general rule, the typical sleeper needs one and a half inches of loft to stay warm at 40 degrees Fahrenheit; two inches at 20 degrees; two and a half inches at zero degrees; and three inches at 20 below zero. Keep in mind, however, that many external factors influence sleep warmth, including dietary fat, general metabolic rate, and body fat. The manufacturers' temperature range classifications are consequently somewhat subjective.

Insulation Material

Experts consider high-quality goose down to be the ultimate in warmth as an insulation in garments and sleeping bags. There have been many recent improvements in synthetic insulation, but goose down, harvested from mature geese during prime months, is still unsurpassed in warmth and comfort. Although goose down is generally considered to be better than duck down, a high grade of duck down can be superior to a low grade of goose down. As the skyrocketing demand for lightweight insulation continues, it is increasingly difficult to obtain high-quality goose down.

Goose down is extremely efficient as an insulating material because of its light weight, its breathability, its compressability, and its resiliency. Some insulators do not breathe as well, or they allow moisture in the form of perspiration and water vapor to pass quickly through the material. Also, down can be compressed into a very small space, as is demonstrated by stuffing a down-filled sleeping bag into a small stuff sack. Its resilient qualities allow it to pop quickly back to its original thickness, even after being compressed for long periods of time. Perhaps as important is the fact that down is the lightest practical insulating material known.

In recent years, polyester and other synthetic fiber insulations have become popular because they have greatly improved in quality, and are much less expensive than down. Polyester material is made from petrochemicals that are extruded into thin fibers about one tenth of the diameter of a strand of hair. When these fibers are crimped and layered into batts, they create loft or bulkiness. The disadvantage of polyester is minimal to the average user. It is a little heavier and not as compressible as down. On the other hand, its major advantage over down is its resistance to moisture. A polyester sleeping bag, for instance, will absorb less than one percent moisture. So, unlike down, polyesters do maintain some loft when wet, and they dry quickly— a real advantage in damp climates. Today Polar-Guard, Quallofil, and

Hollofil II are the most widely used synthetic fiber insulation products, although names such as Hollofil 808, Fortrel, KodOfill, KodOsoff, Primaloft, Thermoloft, and Thinsulate are also common on the market.

PolarGard is made of long continuous strands of fibers, which make very stable nonwoven sheets of material. Hollofil is a short, hollow fiber that, under a microscope, looks like a crinkled tube or garden hose. Quallofil is similar, but each fiber contains four hollow tubes instead of one. This means that the Quallofil fiber is internally reinforced, and this stiffness helps the fiber return to its original shape more quickly than Hollofil or PolarGuard. Also, because Quallofil fibers are relatively short, they compress more easily. In other words, sleeping bags and other garments containing Quallofil are more "stuffable" than those containing most other synthetic insulations.

Bag Construction

One of the primary features of quality and warmth in a sleeping bag is found in the construction of the compartments that hold the insulation material. The best bags are constructed so the inner layer is never stitched directly to the outer layer. The novice is often unaware of this important difference in manufacturing techniques. There are actually five different common techniques of construction used today.

Sewn-through construction is the simplest method of compartmentalizing down and polyester between the inner and outer layers of the shell at regular intervals. The problem with this system of construction is that cold spots occur at the seams where the bag is sewn through, because there is no loft in that area. This method is all right for inexpensive summer bags, but certainly not for those to be used at other times of the year.

The *off-set construction* method can be used by manufacturers of down and polyester bags to compensate for cold spots created from sewn-through construction. This is done by overlapping two layers of sewn-through material so that the seams are alternated.

The other three methods of construction involve the use of baffles in order to minimize uneven distribution of down. These methods are referred to as the *box, slant box,* and *overlapping V-tube* techniques (see Fig. 2.6). The box and slant box techniques involve a series of baffles sewn parallel to one another between the inner and outer walls of the bag. The baffles compartmentalize the down, but do not create cold spots because there are no stitches directly sewn through the bag. The slant box design is considered to be better than the ordinary box design, because the rectangular walls let the down loft better. The overlapping V-tube design is heavier because of its construction, but is the most effective system for retaining uniform distribution of down. This construction consists of small interlocked triangular compartments, which form overlapping V-tubes.

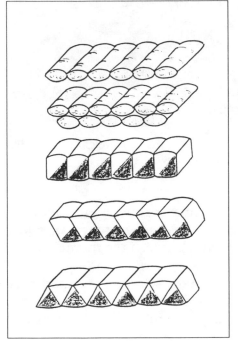

Sewn-through construction

Off-set construction

Box construction

Slant box construction

Overlapping V-tube construction

Fig. 2.6. Construction techniques for compartmentalizing insulation material.

Shape

Shape of the sleeping bag itself has a definite effect on its warmth. Bags are generally classified according to three different styles or shapes. The most popular is the *mummy bag* (sometimes called contour bag), which is cut to fit the shape of the body, thus conserving heat better than other styles (see Fig. 2.7). The bag also has the advantage of being lighter in weight. The mummy provides adequate room for shoulders and arms, but eliminates unnecessary space around the hips and legs. Most have an oval or box-shaped foot.

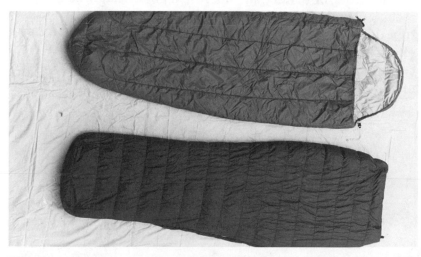

Fig. 2.7. Mummy-shaped sleeping bags. Top: medium-weight polyester bag with hood extension. Bottom: lightweight down bag.

Some persons feel too restricted or confined in a mummy bag, and therefore often prefer the *semi-rectangular model*, which is essentially a compromise between the mummy and a rectangular bag.

Rectangular bags are seldom the selection of experienced backpackers because of the added weight and extra internal space, which absorbs unnecessary amounts of body heat in order to maintain warmth.

Other Features

There are other important factors to consider in selecting a sleeping bag. A good bag will have an extension above the neck, which serves as a hood in cold weather. The hood and shoulder area should have a drawstring that allows the user to tightly close the bag around the head in order to eliminate escaping heat. A snap or velcro closure at the draw hem also allows the bag to be ventilated by opening the zipper; meanwhile the bag is still drawn over the shoulders.

A zipper should run the full length of the bag. High-quality nylon zippers are best, because metal ones cause more heat loss, and often become clogged. The zipper should have pull-tabs at both ends of the bag for easy temperature adjustment at the foot area as well as at the shoulders.

A zipper baffle is another necessary feature (see Fig. 2.8). The baffle is actually an insulated flap inside the bag that extends the length of the zipper closure. Its purpose is to keep the body from coming in contact with the cold zipper and to provide additional protection against the cold.

It is difficult to find one sleeping bag that comfortably satisfies the camping needs of year-round outdoor enthusiasts. A bag that provides adequate protection at temperatures well below freezing will probably be too warm for summer use. The reverse is also true. Hence, when choosing a bag, consider when and where your overnighting is likely to take place. Buy a bag for the coldest use expected and then use its adjustable features—hood, zipper, drawstring—to open the airspaces in order to prevent overheating at warmer temperatures.

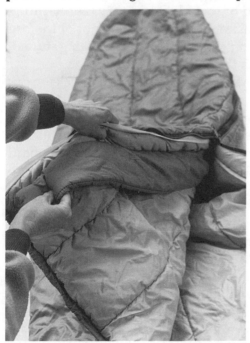

Fig. 2.8. Zipper baffle provides additional insulation on inside of the sleeping bag.

There are very wide differences in how individuals react to cold, but in most cases two pounds of high-quality goose down in a well-constructed bag will be warm enough for temperatures just above freezing. Remember, a bag can always be supplemented by wearing warm clothing inside. In terms of overall bag weight (insulation and material combined), try not to exceed five pounds. For the few engaged in both summer and winter camping, it may be necessary to have both a light- and heavyweight sleeping bag. The majority, however, are able to use a medium-weight bag, which is most adequate for outings during the spring through the fall.

Care of the Bag

A good sleeping bag should last for years if treated with care. The following suggestions will be helpful in handling, cleaning, and storing the bag.

A stuff sack is usually provided with the purchase of a new sleeping bag. The stuff sack serves as a protective cover for the bag, and also keeps the bag compressed in a relatively small space for easy carrying. The bag should always be stuffed into the sack, rather than rolled or folded. Some very tightly-fitting stuff sacks can be filled easiest by inserting the foot of the bag first, which allows air to escape from the bag as it is being stuffed, rather than beginning with the head end.

When the bag is not in use, it is best to store it in a clean, dry place by either hanging or laying it out on a flat surface. If stored in a compressed condition inside a stuff sack for long periods of time, the loft quality of the down or polyester can be reduced.

Washing or dry cleaning down products can be very hard on them. Natural oils and loft of down could be reduced by soap and water. There is also the possibility of interior structure damage, because baffles can easily be torn from the pressure created from water-soaked down. Wash the bag as little as possible. If the nylon cover becomes soiled, wipe it gently with a damp cloth and allow it to dry in the sun. If thorough washing becomes necessary, many authorities suggest using a front loading washer that does not have an agitator. Wash on a gentle cycle, in cold or warm water with a mild soap. The bag should be rinsed several times to be sure all soap is removed. Before lifting the bag, be sure to remove as much water as possible. Allow the bag to dry in the sun, or tumble dry on low heat. If using a dryer, some suggest throwing in a clean tennis shoe to break up the clumped down. When dry, fluff the bag to be sure there are no pockets of down.

A safer alternative to using the washing machine is using a bathtub to launder the bag. Dry cleaning is risky, however, because down can be damaged by strong dry cleaning solvents, which tend to remove the natural oils.

Pads and Matresses

As previously discussed, down or polyester insulation works well when it expands to create a space of still air. Under a person's weight, however, the bottom side of a sleeping bag is compressed to a negligible thickness, creating the necessity to supply some other form of insulation. For this reason, a ground pad is the usual method of providing insulation and comfort (see Fig. 2.9). Such a device is best if waterproof on the underside and, to save weight, three quarters in length (running from shoulders to hips). To protect the head, a stuff sack filled with soft garments works well as a pillow.

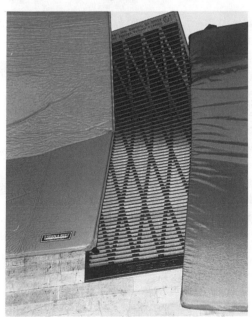

Fig 2.9. Sleeping pads. Left: Therm-a-Rest mattress. Center: Ridge Rest EVA closed-cell foam material. Right: nylon covered open-cell foam pad.

Ensolite, a closed-cell foam, makes an inexpensive but efficient pad, because moisture cannot penetrate its surfaces. Another economical closed-cell pad, Ridge Rest, is one of the most popular mattresses because it has a bit more cushioning. An even more comfortable option is open-cell polyurethane foam, but it does have the drawback of not being water resistant. As a ground pad, it should be 1 1/2 inches thick, and enclosed in a protective shell of waterproof nylon. Also, cotton is desirable on the upper surface of the shell, because it is breathable, does not store up body heat, and lacks slickness.

During mild summer evenings, an air mattress can be used, but because air can circulate within the mattress itself, it is not as warm as a foam pad. Light, short backpacking models take up little room in the pack, but are subject to punctures. However, at least one contemporary brand, Therm-a-Rest, has combined the advantages of open-cell foam mixed with air inside a durable, airtight, waterproof nylon covering. An air valve allows the pad to be deflated and rolled for easy packing. Its insulating properties are much better than a regular air mattress, making this brand the number-one choice among backpackers.

Cooking Equipment and Utensils

Cooking on an open fire and enjoying its warmth during the evening has been a romantic and traditional experience associated with camping. Backpacking and campfires seem almost inseparable. At times, and in the right places, they still are. However, cooking with wood is not always possible, convenient, or, for that matter, desirable. In fact, the advantages of building fires are often heavily outweighed by other factors, particularly their impact upon the land—ashes, charred rocks, and burned grass deposited in fire pits scattered throughout popular campsites. Finding dead wood to burn can also be a problem in heavily used areas, and at high elevations there may be no wood at all. The preferred alternative to cooking over an open fire is using a burner that operates on gas.

Stoves

Modern backpacking stoves are compact and light, ranging in weight from 1 to 3 pounds. A variety of choices are available among several different types. They all save time in cooking, keep pots clean, and eliminate environmental impact problems. They also have a distinct advantage over open fires in that they work in rainstorms.

Fuel

Popular backpacking stoves operate either from liquid fuels, such as white gasoline and kerosene, or from portable fuel canisters containing butane, propane, or a combination of the two. There are yet others that burn alcohol, and there are even a few that consume unleaded gas. The variations seem staggering at first, but are easy to sort out after some additional information.

Stoves that burn white gas or kerosene are more complicated to start, because they operate by converting liquid gas to vaporized fuel. Once started, these stoves automatically heat the fuel to make this conversion. Most, however, must be primed or preheated before they will ignite. For example, the following steps should be followed in igniting several of the popular models that burn white gas.

1. Fill the stove with fuel to about 75 percent capacity, being sure to allow room in the tank for the build-up of vapor.
2. Pressurize the fuel tank by working the pump handle a few times.
3. Insert the cleaning wire or cleaning needle into the gas vent several times to ensure it is clear of soot.
4. Preheat the vaporizing tube by opening the fuel control valve and allowing a small amount of fuel to flow into the cup located just below the burner nozzle. Turn off the valve before igniting the fuel, and allow it to burn until almost out.
5. Open the control valve when the fuel is almost burned off. The liquid gas in the vaporizing tube should now be heated to the point that it becomes vaporized. When the control valve is opened, the fuel should ignite. Even if the fuel is not completely vaporized, there should be enough pressure built up to force liquid fuel through the vent.

This fuel will light and eventually heat the stove until vaporization begins. These steps are not as difficult as they may seem. Once familiar with your own stove, this process becomes second nature.

Similar steps as those just described are used for igniting kerosene burners. However, since kerosene is less volatile than white gas, priming must be done with alcohol.

Gas and kerosene must be handled carefully. Extra fuel should be carried in a metal container designed specifically for that purpose. Round aluminum bottles with a plastic screw cap and rubber gasket are most commonly used (see Fig. 2.10). Be sure to keep the lid on the fuel container at all times except when filling the stove. Also, be certain the stove has cooled before filling and stay far away from any fire source. When filling, use a small funnel or pour spout to eliminate spillage.

Fig. 2.10. Aluminum fuel bottles.

White gas, an additive-free version of auto gas, can be purchased at some service stations. Coleman and Blazo stove and lantern fuel can be substituted for white gas, and can be found in most sporting goods stores. Although a bit more expensive, these fuels are actually considered to be cleaner than white gas, and thus reduce the chance of clogging a stove. Some stoves are shown in Figs. 2.11a-2.11d.

Fig. 2.11 a . Peak 1 Feather 400 white gas stove.

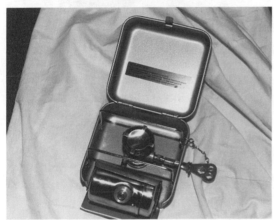

Fig. 2.11 b. Optimus 8R white gas stove.

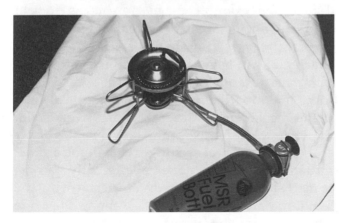

Fig. 2.11 c. MSR Whisperlite International stove burns kerosene or white gas.

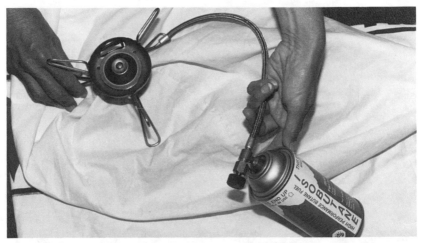

Fig. 2.11 d. MSR Rapidfire Butane stove and cartridge.

A variety of liquid gas stoves are available at mountaineering and outdoor recreation stores. Some of the popular models include Optimus 8R, Svea 123R, Eagle 1000, Coleman Peak 1 Feather 400, and MSR Whisperlite.

Butane and propane stoves are safer and easier to use than white gas stoves. The fuel comes in canisters that look a lot like shaving cream cans, so all you have to do is attach the canister to the burner, turn it on, and apply a match. There is no need to preheat and prime as with the liquid fuel stoves.

There are some negative aspects that often weigh against canister-fueled stoves. For example, the fuels are not as efficient in terms of weight, are much more expensive than white gas or kerosene, and are not always readily available. It is also difficult to know how much fuel you have left in the canister after each use. In addition, butane puts out less heat towards the end of the cartridge and does not vaporize freely at temperatures below freezing. In extremely cold temperatures it can also freeze solid. Propane does vaporize at low temperatures, and operates better in cold weather. Fortunately, fuel cartridges containing a small amount of propane mixed with butane have recently become available on the market, thus increasing the efficiency of butane stoves in high altitude and cold weather. Among the wide selection of butane and butane/propane stoves are the Gaz 470HP, the MSR Rapidfire, and the Primus Trail Scout.

Stove Use

When using the stove, be sure to locate it on a flat surface in a sheltered area away from the wind. A breeze can play havoc with heating efficiency, and can cause the flame to blow out.

On exceedingly hot days, be sure not to allow a fluid gas stove to overheat. Most of these models are equipped with a safety valve located on the filler can that automatically releases when too much pressure builds up inside the fuel container. As gas vapor escapes through the valve, it will likely ignite, shooting a flame several feet into the air. When the pressure is allowed to reduce, the valve will seal and stop the flame. If not, other means must be taken to cool the stove. This may require that you attempt to blow out the flame or, as a last resort, throw dirt or sand on it.

Cooking with the stove inside a tent presents many hazards, and is not recommended unless absolutely necessary. In such a confined space, there is a chance that the stove might tip or be spilled, thus causing fire danger. In addition to fire hazard, there will be depletion of oxygen, build-up of carbon dioxide, and possibly a dangerous exposure to carbon monoxide, if the stove generates very much of this gas. Further, food aromas from cooking can penetrate the tent lining and may attract inquisitive wild animals.

The stove should be used conservatively in order to preserve fuel. Before lighting, have all food preparations ready to place on the flame. Conserve heat and decrease cooking time by covering pots with a lid.

A quart of white gas may be enough for two or three people on a week's outing. Quantities can vary considerably, though, depending on a number of circumstances. Practice and experience will help determine the approximate amount needed. Consideration must be given to the length of the trip, the number of persons sharing the stove, and the types of foods being prepared. Some meals require cooking for 15 minutes or more, while others simply call for bringing water to a boil. Yet another factor to consider is altitude. Cooking time can vary depending on your elevation—the higher you are, the longer it takes to boil water. Cooking time at 10,000 feet is almost three times as long as at sea level.

Other Items

In addition to a campfire or cooking stove, there are a few other items needed to round out the kitchen gear. Selection is as much a matter of personal choice as necessity. From the standpoint of going light and conserving space, you can get by with very little. Following is a limited but adequate list of kitchen accessories for two persons.

> 1 quart-sized pot with lid (ideally, lid has handle to serve as cup or bowl)
> 2 plastic or stainless steel cups
> 2 spoons
> 1 double-bladed pocket knife
> 1 plastic quart water container

There is little need for forks or plates, because most of the meals are eaten with spoons from cups or pot lids. Accordingly, since the single burner stove allows only one preparation at a time, the meals are eaten one course at a time.

Cooking Pots

Aluminum cooking pots are lighter, but many individuals prefer the better heat distribution of stainless steel. If aluminum is used, a thick cooking pot is best, because it is light and provides good resistance to dents. It also tends to heat more evenly. The pot should be designed so that the handle locks in an upright position in order to eliminate burned fingers.

A thrifty alternative is to substitute a small coffee can for the cooking pot. Wire is attached to the rim of the can to serve as a handle, while aluminum foil serves as a lid.

Some campers have difficulty being confined to one pot. Should more than one be needed, a set of nesting pots is handy because each pot fits snugly inside the next larger size for compact storing (see Fig 2.12). Two or three pots with lids should suffice.

Fig. 2.12. Stainless steel nesting cook kit, including clamp handle.

Some pots are marked by notches that indicate levels of measurement. These handy marks can save time and eliminate guessing when mixing foods. For pots that do not already have these measurements, it is quite easy to indicate various levels by etching or scratching marks on the inside of the pot.

Cups

Many backpackers prefer insulated plastic cups, which work well, although some can be subject to absorbing tastes and smells. A few of the die-hard outdoor types still prefer stainless steel drinking cups to ones made of plastic or aluminum. The original stainless steel Sierra Club cup, or at least its prototype, is designed so it can be hung from your belt. The wire handle and the cup rim do not acquire the temperature of hot liquids as do aluminum cups, which are noted for burning lips. The primary disadvantage of the Sierra cup model is its limited capacity and shallow design, which often leads to spilled contents.

Water Containers

Where streams and lakes are frequently located, one small water container may be sufficient to carry. On the other hand, several large jugs may be needed when hiking in the desert, or other places where water is scarce.

The wide assortment of polyethylene bottles available on the market allows ample variety from which to choose. Military-type canteens can also be used. Some popular poly bottles come with attached stoppers and screw lids that virtually eliminate leaks. Even so, some hikers prefer a wide-mouth bottle, which is easy to clean, and convenient for mixing powdered drinks. It is also convenient in cold temperatures, because the lid is less likely to freeze shut.

Food Containers

In addition to hauling water, plastic bottles can be used for packing food. Many varieties of plastic bags, tubes, and jars are also available (See Fig. 2.13). Some are designed specifically for this purpose, while others can be adapted to fit your needs. One handy item is a poly-squeeze tube, which is ideal for holding assortments like peanut butter, powdered milk, or honey. It has a screw cap on one end, and a crimp clip at the other for easy filling. Zip-lock bags are hard to beat, but don't overlook free items, such as discarded plastic bread or produce bags. Containers such as empty shampoo bottles might also be used.

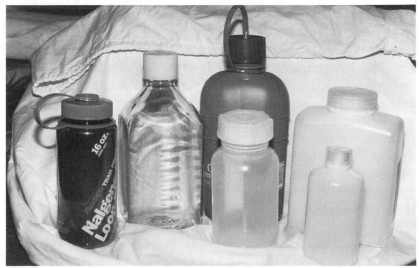

Fig. 2.13. Assorted polyethylene or plastic bottles.

Miscellaneous Kitchen Items

Other eating and cooking gear should be carefully weighed and considered. For instance, plastic or aluminum plates, as well as knife, fork, and spoon sets are available in compact kits. Likewise, lightweight grills, reflector ovens, and teflon fry pans can be selected for open-fire cooking. Compact pressure cookers designed to fit on gas stoves are available for high elevation cooking. The list is unending, so take care to limit the choices wisely to what you really need.

Miscellaneous Equipment

A quick review of the checklist in Appendix D reveals additional items that round out the equipment needs for a safe and enjoyable backcountry trip. Since some of these items (map, compass, sunglasses, water filter, and first-aid kit) are discussed in other chapters, they are not presented here.

Whistle

Hopefully, a small whistle will never really be needed, but just in case someone in your party should ever get lost, this little item can pay big dividends. When traveling in thick woods, it is especially easy to become confused or lost when going even a short distance, and it can turn out to be a very serious matter. As a locating device, a whistle blast carries much farther than the voice, and it can easily be repeated many times.

Flashlight and Candle

A flashlight is not only useful as a matter of convenience, but also can be a valuable safety device in unexpected situations in the middle of the night. Stumbling around in the dark can be a helpless experience. Several compact battery-powered lights, such as those shown in Figure 2.14 a, work well and are available at a reasonable price. Figure 2.14 b shows a model that can be worn on the head, thus freeing up your hands for other things. By using the light only when needed, the batteries will maintain

Fig. 2.14 a. Compact battery-powered lights such as these are popular for backpacking.

Fig. 2.14 b. A battery-powered head lamp such as this frees up hands for other things.

strength for a considerable time. Even so, it is a good idea to carry an extra set of batteries and a bulb in case they are needed.

A small candle projects sufficient light for numerous evening activities and provides a wonderful back-up for the flashlight. Also, a candle is handy for starting wood fires.

Waterproof Matches

Justification for carrying waterproof matches and some other quick means of starting a fire should need little explanation. Nonetheless, many people either forget or don't heed this advice. In addition to carrying a small lighter to quickly ignite a fire under ideal weather conditions, you should also keep several full match containers handy in different locations of your pack. They are also standard equipment for side trips and day hikes as well.

Waterproof matches can either be purchased in outdoor shops, or easily prepared at home. To make your own, simply use stick matches, and melt small amounts of candle wax or paraffin over each match head. For double security, keep matches in a waterproof container, such as a plastic pill bottle or film container.

A word of advice is in order before you purchase waterproof matches. Be sure the match heads are self igniting. Those that must be struck on the side of their container will not work if the container is wet.

Pocket Knife

Many experienced campers carry the Swiss Army Knife, which has a fold-down bottle opener, a screwdriver, and other handy gadgets in addition to two blades. A small pocket knife such as this can serve many purposes, and is much more convenient to pack than a hunting knife. Large-bladed knives, such as those carried in a hip holster, are unnecessary and should be left at home.

Nylon Cord

Braided nylon cord, sometimes referred to as parachute cord, serves many purposes, such as lashing tarp or tent, tying items to the back, hanging food bags in a tree, and building a clothesline. Certainly there are many other ways it can come in handy, such as for extra bootlaces, or for rigging a splint. A total of about 50 feet of 1/8-inch cord in varying lengths should be carried in the pack. The different sizes often come in handy. Nylon cord will fray when cut, so be sure to burn each end in order to fuse the loose braids together.

Toilet Items

In the backcountry it is difficult to maintain the same standard of appearance and cleanliness that we are accustomed to at home, and we shouldn't expect to do so. However, we cannot neglect this area. Hence, each camper should prepare a small bag or kit with such appropriate articles as the following: a small bar or tube of biodegradable soap; a toothbrush, toothpaste, and dental floss; a comb; toilet paper; a polished steel hand mirror; and a washcloth. Depending on individual preference or need, other items might include chapstick, sun lotion, personal medication, etc. Due to its lightness and great absorption ability, a cloth diaper makes an ideal substitute for a washcloth or towel.

Repair Kit

Emergency repair of garments, stoves, packs, and shelters can be aided by having a kit containing the following items: a needle and small roll of thread; several strips of rip-stop tape (for mending holes in tents and down garments); selected cotter pins, both straight and round (for pack frame problems); several feet of rolled wire; and small pliers. A coin could be included, not only to serve as a screwdriver, but also for an emergency phone call at the road head.

Incidentals

Many of the previously-mentioned items in this chapter should be considered as necessities for safe and efficient backcountry travel. On the other hand, there are a few additional things that can be carried along to enhance the pleasure of a trip. Here are some incidentals you might want to take along if space is available in your pack: a camera and film; fishing tackle; a pencil and notebook (for field notes, letters, etc.); field books on birds, animals, geology, etc.; a day pack for short side trips; and binoculars. Carrying any one or more of these items may be considered a sacrifice in weight, but could be well worth it for any gained self-satisfaction and enjoyment.

Unneeded Items

In concluding the section on equipment, this book would be remiss not to mention a few things that are not needed in the backcountry. Items of excess gear would usually include axes, folding saws, and hatchets. They are not needed because most dead timber suitable for burning can be picked up on the ground. Additional items that are definitely not appropriate in the wilderness are transistor radios and portable tape decks. Please leave these kinds of contact with civilization behind.

Footwear

Tremendous stress is placed on the feet when carrying a weighted pack over rough terrain in the backcountry. It is therefore imperative that care be taken to select reliable footwear capable of withstanding such punishment. A poor choice here could lead to any number of difficult situations should the footwear fail far from the trailhead.

Boots

Any backpacking boot should have soles heavy enough to walk over rough, uneven ground without discomfort, but it should not be so heavy that it becomes a drag to lug around. The type of shoes or boots needed depends upon their intended use. For example, a novice might find running shoes most adequate for light walking with a day pack, or even for a short overnight excursion on a fairly level trail. These shoes have their limitations, however, and are definitely not appropriate for cold climates or for rough off-trail hiking. See examples of boots in Fig. 2.15.

Selection

Perhaps the most frequent error made when selecting proper footwear is overbuying; in other words, purchasing boots that are too heavy for the kinds of uses for which they are intended. A few pounds of unnecessary weight on the feet can require a great deal of extra physical exertion over an extended period of time for trail hiking.

Hiking boots are specifically designed for special types of uses. They might conveniently be classified as either hiking boots, trail boots, off-trail scrambling boots, or mountaineering boots. *Hiking boots*, for example, are intended primarily for day

Fig. 2.15. Top: full-grain leather scrambling boots. Center: Gore-Tex fabric/leather upper trail boot. Bottom: low-cut trail shoe.

hiking or short backpacking trips on fairly easy terrain. Hiking boots are light and flexible, and they usually have shallow lug outsoles. Uppers are leather, fabric, or the increasingly popular fabric/leather combination. *Trail boots* are a little heavier, stiffer, and stronger. As would be expected, they are designed specifically for hiking on trails in moderate terrain with a pack weighing up to forty pounds. The upper is supple leather or a robust fabric/leather combination, cut higher for ankle support, and the outer sole is a deeper but flexible lug type. Marginal protection is provided against sharp rocks. *Off-trail scrambling boots,* on the other hand, are medium weight and are usually adequate as all-purpose wear on rough trails or even off-trail in rough country. These boots have more support, thicker soles, and some padding around the ankles. Key characteristics include heavy-duty midsoles, wide outsoles, and above-the-ankle uppers. Many of these boots employ rich, full-grain leather that endures abrasive, wet terrain better than any other material. The toes might also be hardened for protection from rocks, roots, and other objects on rough ground. The majority of backpackers would find these models satisfactory for their outings.

Mountaineering boots amount to off-trail boots with thicker, stiffer leathers and close-trimmed soles for edging on small holds. Half- to full-length steel shanks stiffen these boots for technically demanding travel on alpine rock, snow, or ice. They are designed for very rugged off-trail travel and, consequently, are well beyond the needs of ordinary hikers. These boots are fully padded with hard toes. They are normally too heavy for summer use, but are preferred by a few users for year-round wear. This is often due to the type of terrain in which they are used, as well as the tremendous foot support provided.

Construction

The upper is the portion of the boot above the sole and midsole. It is generally made of leather, but there are variations that include synthetic fabric combined with leather. The highest quality mountaineering and backpacking boots feature one-piece leather uppers with less stitching for water to leak through, and fewer seams to abrade.

Boots should not be too high or be restrictive around the calf. Very high boots give no additional support to the ankle, but can restrict the movement of the calf muscles, and may lead to an irritated Achilles tendon. Most good backpacking boots are from 6 to 7 1/2 inches high, ending somewhere above the ankle bone. Some models also feature a scree shield—a padded elastic collar around the top of the upper—designed to keep out small stones and snow. This option is nice, but not always effective, or for that matter, necessary.

Most boot tongues have a gusset, which is a thin piece of pliant leather sewn between the boot upper and tongue. This structure is desirable, because it effectively excludes moisture and allows the tongue to open wide for removing the boot from the foot.

Careful inspection should reveal that the sole is securely cemented to the upper part of the boot; as an added security on leather boots, this cementing can be backed up with either screws or nails. A rubber (neoprene) lug sole is the standard on most suitable boots (see Fig. 2.16). It should be sturdy enough to retain desirable rigidity, and should grip on varying types of surfaces. Good grip is very important in descending as well as in ascending, because better control is maintained and falls are less likely. The Vibram (a registered trademark) is a very reputable sole found on many boot models.

Fig. 2.16. The sole should be securely cemented to the upper boot. For excellent traction, a rubber lug sole, such as this Vibram brand, is advisable.

In addition to those things already mentioned, there is a variety of other boot features you may wish to investigate, such as strong double-seam stitching for good reinforcing. Also, there are different types of lacings, including eyelets, rings, or hooks, as well as an assortment of other tongue designs. These choices are mostly a matter of personal preference.

Fit

A proper boot fit is as important as design. Be sure that the fit is large enough not to impede circulation or cause chafing at any point. The boot should also be snug enough to give proper arch and ankle support. Any unnecessary foot movement inside the boot can lead to blisters, and can cause toe bruises from constant contact with the front of the boot.

When trying on boots, make every effort to simulate the same conditions that would be encountered in the field. For instance, most hikers prefer to wear two pairs of socks— a light nylon, silk, or poly one next to the foot and a thicker wool pair over it. When fitting boots, be sure to wear both pairs of socks.

To determine proper boot length, follow these simple procedures. Without lacing the boot, kick the toe on the ground or wall and then slide a finger between the heel of the boot and the foot. If you cannot do this, the boot is likely too short. If more than one finger can be inserted, then the boot is too big. Next, kick the heel on the floor (being sure the foot slides to the rear of the boot) and then tie the laces firmly. Now kick the toe. If the foot slides forward enough to touch the front of the boot, you do not have a proper fit. Also, try wiggling your toes up and down and pull them back toward the foot. There should be enough room for free toe movement. With the weight evenly on both feet, the ball of the foot should not be pinched. Also, have someone hold the toe and the heel of the boot rigid while you twist vigorously from side to side. The ball of the foot should fill the boot and barely move; the heel should not move from side to side. Since walking is an important part of boot fitting, be sure to spend plenty of time standing and walking with the boots.

Care and Preparation

Once the boots are selected, be sure they are properly broken in before committing yourself to a long hike. There are several ways of speeding up the process, but the best method is to wear them as much as possible. Begin with short walks at first, and extend the time and distance as comfort allows. Provided the boots are not extremely stiff, the uppers will conform to the irregularities of your feet. It is not uncommon for a new pair of leather boots to require from 30 to 60 miles of walking before they are thoroughly broken in. During this time more than any other, a new owner must be on the lookout for blisters.

There are divergent opinions on the proper methods of boot treatment. The most common procedure is to treat leather with a wax or silicone. Since leather is naturally porous, these compounds will still allow the boot to breathe while providing moderate water-repellent protection. Also, these substances will not soften the leather, and change the structure of the boots. Normally, boot grease or oil should be avoided, because they tend to soften the leather and reduce breathability by closing pores. However, spot treatment may be necessary in order to prevent cracking, and prolong the life of the boot.

Boot seams and welts are vulnerable to water seepage, and stitchings can rot after prolonged exposure to moisture. Application of a thin, narrow coat of AquaSeal Stitch Guard or a good brand of epoxy cement along the seams and welts can help prevent this.

In addition to moisture, another enemy of leather is artificial heat. When boots get wet, always let them dry out at air temperature. Application of heat from a campfire or similar source can cause sole separations, and shrinking and cracking of the leather.

Storing boots properly requires that they be cleaned of mud and dirt. If your boots are wet, stuff newspaper inside them to aid in drying. After they are thoroughly dry, apply an additional light coat of water-repellent material so they are ready for the next outing.

Camp Shoes

In addition to hiking boots, it is often desirable to carry an extra pair of shoes for wear around the campsite. Light running shoes, tennis shoes, or moccasins work well for this purpose. They are comfortable to change into after wearing the boots all day, and this provides a time for wet boots to dry. In addition, hiking boots can be kept dry when crossing streams by wearing camp shoes instead.

Clothing

The wide temperature ranges to which a backpacker might be subjected present difficulties in determining specific clothing needs. The problem is compounded because the type and amount of garments required also depend on the length of the trip, the location of travel, and the season of the year. The choice of garments you carry for warmth, dryness, and shelter deserves your close attention and should be given the highest priority. In recent years there has been an explosion in outdoor clothing fabric innovations, and this has led to some confusion on the part of the beginning backpacker. Some basic suggestions follow.

Dressing for the wide variety of temperatures commonly confronted in the backcountry presents little difficulty if the right combination of clothing is used. Experienced backpackers know the best method of dressing is the layer system. This involves wearing several garments, one on top of the next, rather than one heavy jacket or coat. These several layers of lightweight clothing provide dead airspace for insulation between the fabrics, and allow for proper heat adjustment according to the outside temperature and body heat production.

In addition to insulation benefits, another prime advantage of the layer system is that it helps the backpacker avoid sweating in either cold or hot weather. As is discussed in Chapter 6, the flexibility of adjusting insulation thickness to avoid overheating is extremely important, because the collection of moisture in the form of perspiration can be dangerous in cold temperatures.

The layer system, if used properly during cool temperatures, might include a contact layer made of synthetic fabrics, such as polyester or polypropylene, then a layer of wool or pile followed by an outer layer of nylon. The poly underwear serves to absorb perspiration from the body, the wool or pile adds warmth, and the outer layer of nylon provides wind protection. If the temperature is extremely cold, then added warmth beyond that provided by wool or pile can be obtained by wearing a down or synthetic fiber-filled parka. Rain protection completes the outer layer, if needed.

Moisture absorption will affect the thermal-conductance characteristics of most fibers, so undergarments containing fibers that absorb minimal moisture should generally be chosen for the contact layer. As mentioned, polyester and polypropylene undergarments are designed to transport moisture away from your body along the surface of the fibers, keeping you dry and warm. Natural fibers, such as silk, wool, and cotton, generally do not transport moisture as efficiently as these synthetics. As will be explained shortly, cotton is a particularly poor choice for active wear in cold weather.

Wool and pile are always preferable for mid-layer garments, because they are nonabsorbing fabrics and have the unique property of keeping the body warm even when it is wet. On the other hand, cotton, as with down, provides no insulation when wet, and has high water retention. During exercise, the fabric quickly becomes saturated, clinging to your skin in a cold, clammy embrace. As moisture evaporates in a wet cotton garment, it also draws heat away from the body. This is not only uncomfortable, but also potentially dangerous if heat loss is not slowed or stopped. For these reasons, you should carry at least one wool or pile garment, such as a shirt or sweater. In cold, damp climates, wool or pile pants should also be strongly considered.

In addition to the aforementioned aspects, there are other specific things to look for when choosing garments. Clothing should fit loosely for freedom of movement in the arms, legs, and shoulders; binding in these areas prevents rotation and flex, and causes undue stress. Outer garments need to be large enough to add clothing underneath.

Because there is a need to control body heat and allow perspiration to evaporate, clothing should provide adequate ventilation. Garments should be equipped to open and close with buttons, zippers, snaps, ties, or velcro closures. Such adjustments should be available at the neck, waist, wrists, and front.

A checklist of equipment and clothing that might be desired on a backcountry excursion appears in Appendix D. Certainly not all of those items will be needed for every trip. Therefore, to better judge their desirability, a more detailed description of some of those garments is presented here.

Underwear

As already mentioned, polypropylene or polyester underwear works best in cold and damp climates, because the fabric absorbs almost no moisture and provides good insulation. Reference has also been made to cotton underwear and its major disadvantages in cold, damp climates. On the other hand, in warm, dry environments, cotton is a real treat to have next to your skin when you're not generating excess heat. There is a lot to be said for wearing a cool, damp T-shirt on a blazing 110-degree day. Consequently, in the right climatic conditions, the same kind of underwear worn under your regular clothing may be sufficient for hiking. In any case, for trips of several days' duration, an extra set of underwear should be packed. The extra pair can be washed each day, so a clean change can be made.

Long Pants

Long pants are desirable, to provide not only needed warmth, but also protection of the legs when hiking in thick brush. Pants should be cut full to allow for easy action of the knees and hips, and should be without cuffs. Large pockets with closures are also desirable.

A variety of fabrics are acceptable, but judgment on this should again depend on climatic factors. Wool pants, of course, are highly recommended for hiking in cool, damp areas. Incidentally, good wool pants can be purchased at a reasonable price from army surplus stores; the blue navy pants are particularly popular. Used suit pants are also available from most thrift shops.

Wool tends to wear out quickly, so a mixture of wool and nylon fabric is stronger and more durable. On the other hand, polyesters are lighter and more comfortable for summer use. Blue jeans and other kinds of cotton pants are perhaps most frequently worn, and are all right in good weather, or as long as they stay dry. When wet, they provide little insulation and become quite heavy, so it is important that proper rain protection gear, such as waterproof chaps or leggings, be available in case of rain or snow.

Walking Shorts

Walking shorts provide nice ventilation of excess body heat during hot temperatures and also provide great freedom of leg movement. They are popular in the summer for trail hiking and off-trail travel above timberline. Caution must be used, however, to avoid their use when walking through brush or on sharp rocks. Knee-length knickers without socks also are comfortable, and allow a certain amount of leg ventilation. A word of caution: Because of quick temperature changes in high country, even in the summer, shorts should never constitute the only type of pants.

For comfort as well as for real flexibility in movement and warmth, many backpackers prefer to wear walking shorts in combination with various other garments, such as long-johns, gaiters, and rain or wind pants. Weightier long pants are simply left at home. When the weather turns cold, long-johns are put on under the walking shorts, and gaiters, rain pants, or wind pants are added when needed.

Shirts

As mentioned earlier, at least one shirt or sweater made of wool or pile should be part of your clothing gear. A light button-down polypropylene or polyester shirt or turtleneck can also be worn as an inner layer. Because they can be opened and closed easily for ventilation adjustments, button-down shirts are more advantageous than sweaters. By the way, at least three different polyester fabrics can be used for this layer—Polarlite, Polarplus, and Polarfleece (also called Bunting).

Jacket

If needed, a down, pile, or polyester-filled sweater, vest, or jacket is compact and light, and provides an added layer of warmth. The garment should be waist length with a front zipper or snaps for closure.

Parka

The outer shell for protection against both wind and moisture is usually the hooded parka coat (see Fig. 2.17 a). Likewise, a poncho can also be used to guard against the rain, but it is cumbersome, especially in wind. The parka should be full length, ending well below the waist, with a full-length zipper and overlapping flap with snaps for watertight protection. Velcro closures at the cuffs and a waist drawstring are also desirable.

Fig. 2.17 a. Hooded parka provides protection against both wind and moisture. Gaiters provide a snowproof closure betweeen pant legs and boots.

Actually, the selection of either waterproof or water-repellent fabric for the garment is highly controversial, even among experts, because an assortment of materials are marketed. Waterproof parkas (usually made of a neoprene or polyurethane-coated nylon material) will repel rain or snow, because the material is totally impervious to moisture. For that same reason, however, the garment is not breathable, and therefore accumulates body moisture. In cold weather, there is danger of creating hypothermic conditions from too much moisture build-up, if you are hiking at the time the garment is worn. This is one reason ponchos are still widely used, as air is allowed to circulate under them (see Fig. 2.17 b). If your choice is a waterproof parka, then be sure to take it easy while wearing it.

The ideal rainwear fabric would be completely waterproof from the outside, but would allow all the moisture from the

Fig. 2.17 b. A poncho can also be used to guard against rain.

inside to escape. Presently, a fabric that can do this under all conditions is not available; however, several fabric manufacturers are working on this goal. Until the development of Gore-Tex, there were no claims that breathable, but completely waterproof fabric existed. Waterproof/breathable fabrics are characterized by tiny holes or pores that allow water vapor to pass through the fabric but prevent large water droplets from entering. However, complete wetting of the outer fabric may reduce the breathability of the fabric. Also, cold rain could chill the shell fabric below the dew point, so that moisture from the wearer will eventually condense in the inner layers. Oils and other contaminants also seem to reduce the fabric's waterproofness. In spite of these potential problems, waterproof/breathable fabrics are windproof, offer superior water repellency, and function at least as well as uncoated fabrics under most conditions (1).

One of the best compromises between water protection and breathability has been the parka made of 60/40 cloth (60 percent nylon, 40 percent cotton) and 65/35 cloth (65 percent polyester, 35 percent cotton blend). The tight weave of these fabrics can resist water, but not for prolonged periods of time.

No matter what your choice is for outer protection, be sure to have warm clothing and rain gear readily available, and do not delay the decision to use it as soon as it becomes necessary. Far too many cases of hypothermia occur because backpackers wait too long.

Rain Chaps or Waterproof Pants

Whether using a parka or poncho for protection, there still remains a need to guard the legs from moisture. Either rain chaps or waterproof pants can provide the answer (see Fig. 2.18). They not only keep rain from soaking the legs, but also work well in repelling the morning dew, which accumulates on bushes and tall grass. Actually, chaps are often preferred to rain pants, because they are cooler, covering the legs only. They slip on separately over each leg, and are then tied or snapped to the belt. Urethane-coated nylon chaps are light, and easily stored when not in use. They are available commercially, but can be easily made if you desire to do so.

Fig. 2.18. Rain chaps protect the legs from moisture.

Hat or Cap

Whatever the climate, an appropriate hat or cap should be part of the gear to provide protection from the sun or cold. A stocking cap or balaclava made of wool or a wool substitute is especially important to reduce body heat loss when confronting cold conditions. A balaclava is similar to the stocking cap, but it is long enough to cover the face and neck and provides more insulation (see Fig 2.19). For warmer weather, a billed cap or felt crusher hat is advisable. The crusher hat is a popular choice, because it rolls up to fit into pack or pocket, and reshapes with ease into a variety of looks. It can be soaked with fresh water, and worn to cool the head.

Socks

When discussing boots, it was mentioned that most back-packers prefer to wear two pairs of socks—a light silk or synthetic

Fig. 2.19. Balaclava-style head protection provides warmth for the face, ears, and neck.

one next to the foot, and a thicker wool pair next to the leather. Silk is a slick, slippery liner sock material that works well to minimize chafing and abrasion, but it is not particularly warm when wet. On the other hand, there is also a daunting array of highly-touted synthetic fibers (usually blends of treated nylon, acrylic, or polyester filaments) that provide near-ideal qualities: They absorb virtually no water, wick moisture away from the foot, and remain reasonably warm when soaking wet. Other than that, selection is primarily a matter of personal preference. Most hikers wear short-length socks, which come up only a few inches above the boot itself, although knee-length socks are popular with knickers. Whatever your choice, one extra pair of both heavy and light socks should be carried to allow for a clean, dry change when needed. Soiled socks can be washed each day, and then tied on the outside of the pack for drying along the trail.

Additional Items

When traveling in bug-infested areas, you will appreciate a finely woven headnet to repel mosquitos, black flies, and no-see-ums. Most headnets are light and compact, taking up very little room in your pack (see Fig 2.20). Also, depending on the time of year, there may be a need to consider yet additional items for warmth. Full-length underwear or long-johns, mittens, heavily insulated coats, and perhaps an extra pair of pants would be necessary if hiking in the late fall or early spring or at high alpine elevations. Gaiters or anklets, which provide a snowproof closure between the pant legs and the boots, are essential in winter. Once again, remember to prepare a check sheet of items needed for your outing, and then carefully review your personal needs prior to departing for the backcountry.

Fig. 2.20. Finely woven headnet can provide needed bug protection.

1. Denner, Jon C. A Primer on Clothing Systems For Cold-Weather Field Work , U.S. Geological Survey, Open-File Report 89-415, 1990, 14 pp.

3

FOOD

It is assumed that the majority of those who go backpacking do so for the enjoyment derived from a wide variety of associated activities, including viewing wildlife, taking photographs, going fishing, exploring new areas, etc., and that time spent in meal preparation and cooking is not high on the list of priorities. After all, less time spent in cooking and dishwashing means additional time for more desirable things. This, of course, does not mean there is no concern for proper nourishment and well-balanced diets; it simply implies that we should be aware of the type of meals that are easy and quick to prepare. These remarks are not intended to discourage those individuals who like to do "gourmet" cooking in the backcountry. If that happens to be of great interest to you, simply plan on the extra weight in your pack, and the extra time necessary to do the cooking. If you find that this experience adds to the enjoyment of the trip, then by all means do it.

Selecting Meals

When selecting meals for backpacking, avoid items that come in breakable bottle containers, and heavy foods that contain liquids, such as canned products. Also, to shorten the time spent preparing meals, and to reduce the need to carry an unnecessarily large supply of stove fuel, plan meals that require a minimum of cooking time. Leave out food dishes that are complicated to prepare. In general, any food selected should not require special cooking equipment other than an aluminum or stainless steel pot. After all, these one-pot meals can be filling, cheerful, and easy to cook.

Most experienced backpackers select a lunch menu that requires no cooking, and thus eliminates the time and energy needed to perform related tasks. On the other hand, breakfast and supper meals usually should include something warm. As a matter of expediency, however, the breakfast should not be too elaborate if the group expects to get an early start on the trail. Bacon, eggs, pancakes, and frying pans are luxuries most experienced persons leave at home; high-protein cereals make a more efficient breakfast for backpacking, and save time in clean up. If any meal is to be time-consuming to prepare, let it be the evening dinner; its pace can be more relaxed, because you know that your destination for the day has already been reached.

It is easy to get by with only 1 1/2 to 2 pounds of food per person per day in the backcountry. Modern freeze-dry and dehydration techniques have greatly reduced the overall weight of food products, by taking most of the original moisture out of them. This means the moisture that is eliminated need not be carried in the pack; it is simply added to the food in the form of water once you reach your destination. This accounts for a tremendous savings in weight, and dehydrated and freeze-dried products are tasty, compact, and unspoilable. In most cases, all that is required to prepare them for eating is to add the proper amount of boiling or cold water and let the food rehydrate for a few minutes according to the instructions.

Most of the freeze-dried dinner products are packaged in plastic pouches or foil trays from which the food can be both prepared and eaten. Many different fruits, vegetables, and meats are available in freeze-dried form. Some of the more familiar companies producing these quick food products are Mountain House, Richmoor Natural High, Backpacker's Pantry, AlpineAire, and DriLite Foods. Sporting goods stores and mountain shops carry a wide range of these products, and they are also sold through most outdoor equipment catalogs. Two of the largest outfitters, Campmore, Box 997, Paramus, New Jersey, 07653-0997, and Recreational Equipment Inc., P.O. Box 88125, Seattle, Washington 98138-2125, carry some of these foods, and sell them through the mail.

For trips of short duration, especially when weight may not be so important, retort foods can also be taken along. "Retorts" are pre-cooked foods that are vacuum sealed in foil pouches. The retort pouch seals in the flavor of entree ingredients, such as meat, vegetables, and spices, so all you have to do is heat the pouch in boiling water and serve.

Those specialized food products found only in sporting goods stores are more expensive than regular foods, because the techniques involved in their production are more time-consuming and involved. Even so, low-cost lightweight foods suitable for outdoor cooking can be found in food markets and specialty food stores. Economy-minded backpackers who don't mind a little extra work can create their own combinations from the various packaged foods and instant soups on supermarket shelves. By carefully selecting and combining lower priced items with the more expensive backpacking specialties, you should be able to greatly reduce the overall cost of your food. Of course, the length of the backpack trip is a factor to consider when selecting food products. For trips longer than three or four days, you will want to use more of the concentrated, dehydrated, and lightweight foods; for shorter trips, you may prefer to carry some of the regular staples used at home.

A low-cost way to keep your pack light and still eat well in the woods is to dehydrate your own food at home. By doing so, you can create nearly any menu you want on a trip. For thousands of years, people have dried foods to preserve them for later enjoyment, and many of us are still doing it. You can dry almost any kind of fruit, vegetable, or meat. Once in the backcountry, these dried foods can be combined with staples such as rice, beans, cereal, and cheese to enliven any meal. Perhaps the best way to use dried vegetables is in soups and stews.

Drying food is simple and easy to do. How does it work? Bacteria, yeast, and molds can live only when foods contain a certain amount of moisture. Removing moisture from the food helps to prevent decay, and reducing the water content to 25 percent or less helps to preserve food.

By the way, the nutritional value of dried food is about equal to that of frozen food. Four pounds of fresh food will give you approximately one pound of dried food, but because the water is missing, you end up with highly concentrated food, containing more food value pound for pound than fresh food. Air, moisture, and sunlight are the enemies of dehydrated food, but when stored properly, it will last several years.

The many drying options include the use of ovens, food dehydrators, solar dryers, and simple homemade dryers. Using your own oven or a less efficient homemade dehydrator will likely do just fine, but serious backpackers should consider a commercial model. Most of the commercial dryers come with a beginner's manual that specifies temperature details, drying times, pre-drying treatments for some foods, and even recipes. More advanced books are available at most libraries, or through bookstores.

Counting Calories

Unfortunately, no formula can be completely accurate in determining the necessary number of calories needed for any one person on a given backpack trip, because there are simply too many variables relating to our energy requirements. On the average, the daily caloric output for a backpacker could range between 4,000 and 6,000 calories, and by the end of a very strenuous day it is quite possible that a person could easily use 7,000 to 8,000 calories. By comparison, the average person living in a city and doing office work might burn less than 2,000 calories in a day.

It is possible to calculate the approximate number of calories you need each day, and this can be very helpful in determining how much food to take on an extended outing. Ascertaining how much food will be needed depends on your body size, and how much hiking or similar forms of exercise you plan to do. Table 3-1 can help you figure your needed calories (1). Simply add the basic calories used per day by multiplying your body weight by 10. This sum equals the number of calories used in a day of hiking.

For example, a 165-pound adult carrying a 44-pound pack for five hours would use: 4.02 (from chart) X 165 (body weight) X five (hours) = 3,317 (hiking calories). 165 (body weight) X 10 = 1,650 (basic calories). Hiking calories plus basic calories equals 4,967 calories per day.

For a short trip of two or three days, we actually could give minimal consideration to a balanced diet, as long as we are in

Table 3-1
Calories Used in Hiking

Pack weight	Calories per hour per pound of body weight	Hiking calories
No pack	3.30	x body weight x hours of hiking = hiking calories
11-lb. pack	3.54	x body weight x hours of hiking = hiking calories
22-lb. pack	3.84	x body weight x hours of hiking = hiking calories
44-lb. pack	4.02	x body weight x hours of hiking = hiking calories

Hiking calories   =   _____

Body weight x 10 = + _____

Calories needed   =   _____

reasonable health to begin with. A well-nourished person can go for a week or more on the barest of diets with little difficulty. Even for short outings, however, we must consider the need for carbohydrates and fats, which provide quick replenishment of energy to meet the increased demands on our body. When an outing is to last for an extended period of time, such as a week or more, then nutrition intake becomes even more important to consider. Fortunately, most trail foods have at least some nutritional value. Inexperienced hikers are seldom bothered by not having enough food to eat; the common tendency is to take too much.

Since no formula can be completely accurate in determining our specific individual food needs, about the only way to tell whether we are eating enough of the right things is to get some idea of the calories consumed, and then monitor how we feel throughout the trip. Trial-and-error experience on short hikes will help determine the amount of food needed.

Balancing the Diet

The vitamins and minerals taken through normal meals are usually sufficient to meet daily needs. If there is any doubt that your diet is providing your daily requirements, supplement it with common multiple-vitamin capsules. On the other hand, backpacking menus, particularly for long trips, should be properly balanced with three essentials for energy—proteins, carbohydrates, and fats. Proteins keep the body in good working order, because each day it must rebuild itself. An inadequate amount of nutrients, especially protein, prevents the rebuilding from being completed and leads to the gradual deterioration of the body, starting with the muscles. Accordingly, carbohydrates and fats provide sources of energy for the body. Fats are necessary for long-term energy needs, while carbohydrates provide the quick reserve of energy for work beyond our normal level.

Carbohydrates

Carbohydrates are the body's most efficient source of energy, so active backpackers need to eat plenty of this kind of food. The carbohydrates you eat are converted to glycogen, which is stored in the muscles and liver. When you exercise, your body calls on these glycogen reserves to give you energy. Unlike fats or protein, carbohydrates can be used by the body during any phase of exercise. Dried fruit, vegetables, whole grains, cereals, legumes, and milk products are all excellent sources of carbohydrates.

Fats

As mentioned, after you have been continually exercising for a long period of time, your body begins to burn its fat reserves. Fats are the most concentrated food source of energy, having more than twice the calories as proteins or carbohydrates, and they "burn" more efficiently and last longer than carbohydrates. Even though fat intake is important, bear in mind that for health reasons it should be eaten in moderation. In fact, under normal circumstances, fats probably should not compose more than 20 to 30 percent of daily caloric intake. Sources of fat that might be included on a backpack trip include margarines, oils, cheese, nuts, chocolate, canned fish, and the like.

Protein

There seems to be a great deal of confusion about protein, which is the building block of body tissue. Simply stated, it is needed to make your body grow. It can also be used as an energy source, although it does so only as a last resort when no carbohydrates or fats are available. When your body begins to burn protein, your muscles and other body components suffer.

While you need protein to have muscle tissue, you don't build bigger muscles simply by increasing your intake of protein. Regular exercise of specific muscle groups *and* more calories will increase muscle mass and strength. You should know, however, that the added calories need to come from protein, carbohydrates, and fat—not just protein. In other words, vigorous exercise, such as hiking, increases the body's need for calories, but not calories derived only from protein.

For healthy adults, the recommended dietary allowance is 0.36 grams of protein for each pound of ideal body weight. If your ideal weight is 175 pounds, you need 63 grams of protein per day. If your ideal weight is 125 pounds, you need 45 grams of protein each day (2). Americans typically eat twice the amount of protein they need. Provided you eat a balanced diet, you do not need more than 15 to 20 percent of your daily calories from protein. If you consume extra protein beyond this amount, it most likely will end up as uninvited body fat.

Examples of protein foods suitable for backpacking are canned, dried, or cured meat, fish, and poultry; dairy products, such as cheese and powdered milk; eggs; and various plant foods such as dried beans, nuts, seeds, potatoes, pasta, rice and corn. When planning which foods to take, it is helpful to know that animal products—eggs, milk, fish, poultry, and meats—are called "complete" proteins because they contain all of the essential amino acids required for our bodies to utilize the protein. "Incomplete proteins," on the other hand, come from plant foods, which are low in one or more of the essential amino acids. Consequently, before consuming plant foods, it is important that you use the following two simple rules to combine the right foods to make nutritionally complete proteins:

1.   Combine any legume (dried beans or peas, peanuts, or soy-based food) with any nut, seed, or grain (for example, wheat, oats, corn, or rice). A good old peanut butter sandwich is a great example.
2.   Combine any grain, legume, nut, or seed with small amounts of milk, cheese, yogurt, eggs, bread, meat, fish, or poultry. Examples include oatmeal with powdered milk, macaroni and cheese, rice pudding, pancakes, potatoes au gratin, tofu burgers on bread, and Spanish rice.

General Considerations

Because of the body's continual need to replenish itself with calories, the backpacker should eat throughout the day, rather than separate meals into the three distinct time segments of breakfast, lunch, and supper. To ensure that the body receives continuing nourishment, snack along the trail between regular meals. This continuous refueling of the body system will keep the energy level high throughout the day.

Of all energy foods for snacking, "gorp" is by far the most popular among backpackers. If the contents of this food are mixed properly, there is a good balance of protein, carbohydrates, and fats. The carbohydrates provide quick energy, while the fats and proteins are absorbed more slowly to provide lasting power. Nuts, seeds, and dried fruits are traditional ingredients. Other good additions are roasted soybeans or roasted wheat, which when combined with nuts, make a complete protein. Although the variations in recipes for this concoction are almost endless, following is one popular blend.

1 cup salted peanuts
1 cup raisins
1/2 cup coated chocolates, such as M & Ms
1/2 cup mixed nuts

Any other haphazard mixture of nuts, seeds, candy, raisins, dried fruits, and granola cereal will likely be just as enjoyable as this recipe. Substitute dried fruits for candy whenever possible, because the fruits supply nutrients and satisfy your sweet tooth at the same time. Gorp can be eaten by the handful whenever the body gives signs of needing a little extra fuel.

To properly prepare for an outing, make written menu plans for each meal before purchasing the food. It is also helpful to be familiar with any new recipes by trying the meal at home before attempting to prepare it on the trail. This should be done not only to know whether you like the food, but also to be sure of the quantities. For example, some freeze-dried packets marked as servings for two persons are often only adequate for one.

Most dry foods purchased in paper boxes or glass containers should be repacked in plastic bags before the outing. By doing so, you eliminate weight and space and take only the desired amount needed for the trip. When repackaging, be sure to cut the recipe from the box and put it in the food bag. Also, to save time in the field and to simplify preparation, try premixing recipes at home; combine any dry ingredients that are to be cooked or served together. For instance, if you like sugar and powdered milk with your coffee, then add the proper amounts to your coffee supply while readying the food for the trip.

For final packing, it is recommended that all items be put together in large bags according to the three meals of the day. Consequently, all food for breakfast, lunch, and supper is bagged separately and then labeled accordingly. This prevents the need to sort through all the grub while looking for specific meal items. It is also handy to have a fourth bag that contains any common items such as salt, coffee, sugar, and similar things that are used at several different meals.

Menus and food preferences depend a great deal upon individual choices and appetites. Through trial-and-error you will soon learn what is best for you. The following menu selections for a full day's outing are simple, easy, and quick to prepare, because mixing with cold or boiling water is all that is required.

BREAKFAST

Instant coffee, tea, or hot chocolate
Instant oatmeal, granola, or cold cereal with raisins

LUNCH

Hard crackers with peanut butter, salami, or cheese
Gorp (also for snacks throughout the day)

SUPPER

Soup
Macaroni and cheese or stew of your choice
Instant coffee, tea or hot chocolate
Instant pudding with rehydrated fruit

EXTRA INGREDIENTS
Salt
Sugar
Powdered milk

For a more complete list of various foods that can be considered for alternative menus, see Appendix E.

1. The original source of this chart is "The Good Food Store's Portable Pantry," The Good Food Store, 1981, 4 pp. This source also provides other pertinent information relative to nutrition and backpacking foods.
2. This recommendation is set by the Food and Nutrition Board, a national group of nutritionists and scientists, and is intended to be generous.

4

NAVIGATION AND TRAVEL TECHNIQUES

Route finding and navigation techniques require considerable study and practice in the field in order to develop necessary competencies. Once learned, freedom and self-sufficiency to roam the backcountry with ease are the rewards. To do so, however, we must know something of navigational tools and their uses, as well as other means of determining routes, distances, and direction of travel.

Maps

Maps play an important role in backcountry navigation. Once experienced in their use, you can venture forth with the confidence needed to leave the crowd and the beaten path. Many backcountry users lack the understanding and ability to go anywhere except where the trail leads. If you really want to be able to reach that unnamed lake or find an area seldom seen by human eyes, you must learn to read maps. They give you the ability to determine your own routes, and get away from dependence upon trails to get your party where it wants to go.

To adequately master the skills of map reading, you must practice in the field at every opportunity. There simply is no substitute for the real thing— the opportunity to compare map images with real ground features.

Among the maps used most in the backcountry, topographical maps (often referred to as "topos" or "quads") are the most valuable. The best topographical maps available are prepared by the United States Geological Survey (USGS). The U.S. Forest Service and Bureau of Land Management recreation maps are also valuable supplements for determining locations of logging roads and other access routes to the trailhead. These maps are revised more frequently than the USGS maps, and consequently the information about roads and trails can be more up to date.

Obtaining Maps

Indexes showing topographic maps published for each state are available upon request from the U.S. Geological Survey. Each state index identifies each map quadrangle by name, and the catalog shows which ones are available, and the year each was published. Also available is a free USGS brochure, "Topographic Map Symbols," which explains the map scales and symbols used on topos. To order maps, the USGS brochure, and individual state indexes and catalogs, contact the USGS Map Sales office in Denver, Colorado (the address is listed in Appendix B). Each 7.5-minute map costs $2.50. In addition, you can buy maps over the counter at USGS offices and state-operated Earth Science Information Centers at the locations listed in Appendix B. Also provided in that appendix are addresses for obtaining maps and related information from other sources.

Reading Map Information

The space in the margins of a map is normally used to identify and explain the map, providing information such as how the map was made, what location it covers, and when it was constructed. Also provided is information on the map scale, the distance in elevation between contour lines, the magnetic declination from true north, and the name of the quadrangles adjacent to the map.

Scale is the relationship or ratio between distance on the map and actual distance on the earth's surface. Scale is usually expressed in the form of bar scales, ratios, or words and numerals. USGS maps, for example, usually provide separate bar scales for feet, miles, and kilometers.

Learning to use bar scales is easy. A piece of paper can be used to mark the distance between two points on the map. Then by placing the paper on the bar scale, one can read the total distance between the points.

The ratio method expresses the scale in the form of a fraction. As an example, a fraction of 1:24,000 means that one unit of measure on the map is equal to 24,000 of the same unit on the ground. Words and numerals, when used to express scale, are usually in some convenient unit of measure, such as 1/2 inch = one mile.

The USGS topographic maps found to be most popular among backpackers are at a scale of 1:24,000. On such maps, one inch equals 2,000 feet, which is about 2.6 inches to a mile. Maps to this scale are called 7.5-minute maps, because they cover that many minutes of longitude and latitude. One map at this scale will cover from 49 to 70 square miles, and is of sufficient detail to determine contour changes and other related information. About 55,000 of these maps are needed to show the entire United States.

From 1910 to about 1950, maps showing an area within 15 minutes of latitude and longitude were the USGS standard for topographic coverage of the United States. These 15-minute maps, scaled at 1:62,500 (one inch = about one mile), are not as easy to read, because the details are smaller. The area within one of these maps is equal to 197 to 282 square miles. Some of these maps are still available, particularly for the few places not yet covered by the now standard 7.5-minute maps.

Topographical maps use lines and symbols to represent various features. A valuable characteristic of these maps is the portrayal of the shape and elevation of the terrain by contour lines. They show surface configuration with a sense of three-dimensional relief (see Fig. 4.1). These lines on a map follow the ground surface at a constant elevation above sea level. If you were able to follow a contour line while walking, you would never go uphill or downhill, and eventually you would return to your starting position after going completely around a hill. These lines are shown on the map as thin brown lines that connect points of equal elevation on the ground. By use of contour lines and their relationship to one another, a map reader can interpret

Fig. 4.1. Contour lines on a map show surface configurations with a sense of three-dimensional relief. This segment of a topographic map shows contour lines at 20-foot intervals and also reveals common symbols used to represent various features.

the general shape of the landscape. With practice, you can learn to read contours in determining the height of hills, depth of valleys, and elevation and slope of the ground at any point.

A graphic representation of contour lines and how they work can be illustrated by stacking five or six books on top of your desk. The largest book should be on the bottom and each additional book should be stacked on top of the larger book in descending order of size. These stacked books will represent a mountain. Looking at the stack of books from the side, you can now imagine that each book represents one contour line; each is level and parallel to the others. Now look at the stack of books from the top. You will see a series of descending steps. The steps will be closer together where the pitch of the rock is the steepest, and farther apart where the pitch is shallow. This same system works in determining the steepness of a mountain by reading the contour lines on a map. Where the contour lines are very close together, the terrain is steep. Where the contour lines are far apart, the terrain is gentle or level.

If the contour lines of a particular mountain are generally

circular and about the same distance apart on all sides, then you know the mountain will be shaped like a cone or rounded hump. Two small series of circles located at the center of a contour line would represent twin peaks. If the contour lines on one side of the mountain are far apart but close together on the other side, then the mountain has one gentle slope to the top, and a sheer or steep slope down the other side. If your goal is to reach the top of the mountain, you will obviously find the gentle slope to be the easiest route.

When examining trails or planning cross-country routes, you will be going up or down whenever your route crosses contour lines. The vertical distance between each line is known as a contour interval. Most maps have the contour interval printed in the map legend or under the map scale. The distance in elevation between contour lines on a given map depends on the chosen scale and on land relief. A small contour interval is used for flat areas; larger intervals are used for mountainous terrain. To determine the number of feet of change in elevation, simply count the number of contour lines between two points, and multiply by the contour interval shown on the map.

The distance between contour lines on many USGS 7.5-minute topographical maps is either 20 or 40 feet. Also, every fifth contour line is heavier in print for easy distinction, and is labeled with elevation figures. Thus, on maps using 20-foot contour intervals, the elevation distance between each heavy line represents 100 feet.

Getting Additional Information from Maps

Here are a few additional hints and some words of caution before leaving the topic of maps. First, keep in mind that map revision does not always keep pace with such changes in features as new roads, trails, buildings, and reservoirs. Also, errors do crop up now and then in maps. Today most maps are compiled in the office by photogrammetric methods using aerial photographs taken thousands of feet above. As a result, errors in interpretation of features are possible, even though material is double checked on the ground by persons knowledgeable about the area. For example, a well-developed game trail could possibly be misinterpreted by mappers as an official trail, and could therefore be so designated on a map. Should you select that trail as your means of reaching a destination, you may end up bushwhacking to get there.

Take advantage of high altitude when attempting to match your map with existing landmarks. You are at a distinct advantage in viewing peaks, valleys, lake pockets, and other features from such a location. Once you return to low elevation, such as a valley floor, it is possible to lose sight of easily distinguishable landforms, due to topography in the foreground that blocks your view.

When determining hiking miles from a designated trail on a topographical map, keep in mind that actual trail distance is often longer than designated. This is due to the fact that small irregularities are not always shown. For example, small switch-backs may not be printed on the map. Some experienced hikers suggest that a way to approximate true mileage is to add to the length of the trail on the map an additional 20 percent of the distance where no switch-backs exist, and 100 percent where there are many switch-backs.

Practice your map-reading skills by comparing the map with what you see on the ground. When you are able to match map formations and real terrain in your head, you have mastered the art. This can only come about by constant repetition in the field.

The Compass

A skilled map reader equipped with a good topo map may not often need to use a compass for navigation because, with practice, learning to recognize existing terrain and other landmarks as shown on the map is not difficult. There are occasions, however, when compass skills become important, particularly when one becomes disoriented or seeks to identify an unrecognizable landmark or specific location. A compass also is helpful when navigating during times of poor visibility, such as in fog, heavy snowfall, or darkness.

In using the compass, keep in mind that the needle responds to the earth's magnetic pull and always points to the magnetic north pole, where the polar field is located. Unfortunately, the polar field is located approximately 1,000 miles south of the geographic north pole, and, as a result, a compass reading does not automatically tell us the direction of true north. To be accurate in the use of map and compass, we must therefore compensate for any deviation between magnetic north and true north. Not accounting for the variation could cause enough error for us to miss a destination point.

The deviation or angle of variation between true and magnetic north is referred to as magnetic declination (see Fig. 4.2). In the United States, those living on the west side of the line of zero declination (called the agonic line) will have an easterly declination. In other words, magnetic north will be to the east of true north. The opposite is true for those living to the east of the agonic line. Also, depending on geographic location, the amount of east or west declination will vary. For example, the declination angle in Montana can be 20 degrees east and in Maine 21 degrees west.

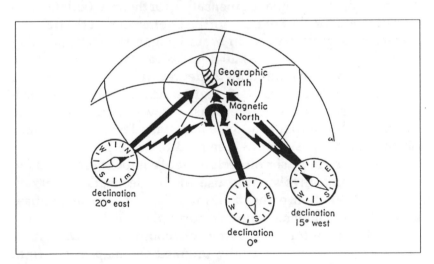

Fig. 4.2. Angle of declination varies depending upon geographic location from the geographic north pole and magnetic north.

All Geologic Survey maps, as well as many produced by other agencies, provide information on magnetic declination. USGS topographic maps have declination diagrams at the bottom margin, which consist of two lines joined in a triangle. The vertical line with a small star at the top is representative of true north, while the line forming an arrow pointing to the letters "MN" reveals the direction of magnetic north. Also provided is the number of degrees of magnetic deviation. A third line on the diagram is marked "GN" for grid north. We are not concerned with this, because its use is for a coordinate system of navigation.

Simple steps can be followed when orienting a map to true north. Keep in mind that there are several different techniques that can be used in addition to the ones described here. Also, since there are several different compass models on the market, you should be sure to read any specific instructions provided with your own.

The first step in orienting the map is to lay it out on a flat surface; attempt to compare the actual features you can see with the same features shown on the map. The second step is to orient the map using the compass. This is done by lining up the map with the compass pointing to magnetic north. Then, in order to compensate for effects of declination, rotate the map and the compass together, while compensating for the specific degrees of variation east or west of true north. For instance, if the declination is 20 degrees west, you would rotate the map (simultaneously with the compass) 20 degrees east of magnetic north. Essentially you are subtracting 20 degrees from 360 degrees. The compass would then read 340 degrees. Conversely, if the declination was shown as 10 degrees east, you would turn the map 10 degrees west, in order to add the necessary degrees to magnetic north. The compass would then read 10 degrees.

Perhaps a more simple technique of compensating for magnetic deviation involves the use of the declination diagram located at the bottom of the USGS map. Simply align the compass along the line showing magnetic north (the one that is an arrow with "MN" at the top). By having your compass set towards true north, you have automatically oriented the map in the right direction(see Fig. 4.3).

Once the map is properly oriented and your position is determined, it becomes easy to identify ground details by comparing map bearings with field bearings. For example, you might wish to confirm that a mountain peak in the distance is the one you have marked on your map to reach. To do so, place the compass on your present position on the map and sight it toward the mountain peak. If the peak is shown on the map, it will be found along that bearing. Be sure to examine all elevation features along the bearing, to be sure that a low ridge in the

Fig. 4.3. Using the declination diagram at the bottom of the map, notice that an easy method of compensating for magnetic deviation is to align the compass along the line showing magnetic north ("MN"). If the compass is set toward true north, as shown here, the map is automatically oriented in the right direction.

foreground does not block the view of the proper peak. Such errors are common to persons not experienced in the use of map and compass.

Now if you wish to walk this bearing in order to travel to the selected mountain peak, it would not be practical to hold the compass on the chosen direction while hiking. Instead, using the compass, select a distant landmark or a spot in the direction you want to go. Walk to that spot without looking at the compass and then repeat the procedure.

Another use of the compass is to find your exact location on a map. This is done by taking back bearings on at least two known land features that are identifiable on the map. The bearings will be taken from the place where they will intersect—at your exact location. To plot these intersections on the map, first select two recognizable land features, preferably close to 90 degrees apart. These features must also be recognizable on the map. Then take bearings on these two features and compute their back bearings. A back bearing is computed by figuring the opposite direction of the compass reading. Simply subtract or add 180 degrees to the original bearing. Next, using the side of your compass as a straight edge, connect the points by drawing lines on the map in accordance with the known back bearings. Your position on the map is where the two lines intersect.

There is one final important note on the subject of the compass—trust it! In times of confusion over direction, it is sometimes difficult to believe what your compass is telling you. The chances are that the compass is right and you are wrong.

Other Means of Determining Direction

There are other means besides the use of a compass to determine direction in the outdoors. These methods should not be considered as routine substitutes for the valuable compass, however. The compass should always be a part of your standard gear.

The stars are our oldest and most faithful guides to direction. You can locate the North Star by finding the Big Dipper and the Little Dipper in the sky. The two stars opposite the handle that form the front edge of the Big Dipper are known as the "pointers" because they point directly to the North Star in the tip of the Little Dipper's handle. Although the Big Dipper circles around the Little Dipper every 24 hours, the pointers never cease pointing to the North Star.

True south can be found with an old-fashioned dial watch. Point the hour hand directly at the sun. The point halfway between the hour hand and twelve o'clock is south. Hold the watch level when doing this, and also be sure it is set on standard time.

Another method of using the sun to determine direction is to push a stick into the ground in an open area where you can see its full shadow. Mark the end of the shadow with a small stake or rock. Wait 15 minutes or so, and again mark the end of the new shadow position. By scratching or marking a line between these two markers you will have an east-west line. The first marker represents west. Drawing a tangent from the stick to this line will give you north. This method is accurate enough to get you going in the right direction should you be disoriented.

We should keep in mind that the sun alone can provide us with a general sense of direction, because it is common knowledge that it rises in an easterly direction and sets in a westerly one. But in case of clouds or fog, we can also look for other factors that might provide valuable assistance in determining direction. Knowledge of characteristics unique to your own geographic area can be helpful. For example, in the mountains it is common to find snowfields on the north and east slopes where the sun does not reach. Also, south and west slopes, due to being sunnier, are more likely to reveal growth representing dry habitat vegetation.

Altimeter

An additional dimension that can be helpful in orienteering in mountain country is a pocket altimeter. Such a tool is not mandatory equipment, but it can be very handy in determining your exact location on a map. When using an altimeter, you must remember to set it every day because it is the same as a barometer in that it reacts to changes in pressure caused by the movement of weather systems. This means you must set the altimeter to a known altitude at the beginning of the trip and, having established where you are from time to time on the trip, set it to the altitude shown by the contour lines on your map. The beauty of an altimeter is that you can almost always pinpoint precisely where you are on the trail. This is done by taking an altitude reading off the altimeter, and then finding that altitude on your trail by using the contour lines of the map.

Time/Distance Estimation

How long will it take us to hike a mile? Can we reach our next campsite before dark? These and other time/distance questions are frequently asked by inexperienced backpackers. A commonly used method of estimating the time a hike should take is to allow one hour for every three miles of distance on flat terrain, plus an additional hour for every 1,000 feet of steep ascent or descent.

Let's apply this method to the following example. Your map shows that there are six miles of trail to the next campsite. By counting contour lines on the map, you are also able to determine that the trail climbs 1,500 feet, and then descends 500 feet before your destination. The formula reveals that it will take you four hours to reach your next camp (six miles = two hours + 2,000 feet of ascent and descent = two more hours).

The time/distance formula, of course, should be varied somewhat, depending upon your own hiking speed. Experience allows you to adjust the calculation for more accuracy. Be sure to allow for additional time if you take rest stops.

Orientation to the Trail

Trail navigation does not end with mastery of techniques used to determine direction and elevation on maps. There are still other skills that must be applied for proper trail orientation.

Many of the official trails built and maintained by state and federal agencies are identified at the trailhead by name or number. It is not uncommon for land managers to post additional trail information near the starting point, such as signs showing distances to various points of interest. Also, a number of wilderness and backcountry areas will provide registration boxes with instructions for signing in your party prior to beginning the trip.

Accommodations such as those just mentioned are not always available, however. At times there can be difficulties in actually finding the trailhead prior to beginning the trip, let alone knowing if you are on the designated trail once underway. Much of our entry to hiking areas comes from rustic logging roads built into forested areas. As new timber cuts take place, these roads are expanded and changed, resulting in relocation of trailhead access points. In other cases, trailhead markers are left in a pile of rubble.

There are yet other factors that create difficulty in trail orientation. For instance, in many designated wilderness areas, distance and direction signs are no longer routinely located at trail junctions. Also, in some cases old trail maintenance standards have been changed in order to allow trails to return to a more natural state, and to reduce their obtrusiveness on the land. As a result, vegetation growth and downed timber can conceal trailheads and routes. In such circumstances it becomes easy to either lose the trail altogether, or to mistakenly leave it while unknowingly following a well-worn game trail. Orientation cues in the backcountry are not always distinctive, unless you pay attention and become a close observer. Hence, knowledge of other techniques used to recognize trail routes is valuable.

One method used by experienced mountaineers to identify forest trails is to look for tree blazes. A blazed trail has strips of bark cut from individual trees every so often along the route of travel. These bark strips or notches have been cut with an axe or hatchet and are usually located on tree trunks approximately at shoulder height. The cut is generally uniform in size, being five or six inches long. A well-established blaze may also have a smaller notch located just above the longer one. This double blaze is easier to distinguish from a tree scar that might have been caused by disease, impact from a nearby fallen tree, or some other means.

Blaze marks can be recognized for many years, as is demonstrated by the fact that some older trees still have visible marks made decades ago by Native Americans and explorers. It is exciting to come across these reassuring trail signs in the wilderness, but good practice today does not allow us to create our own blaze marks. Not only is it unnecessary to deface timber, but also the feeling of solitude or adventure is broken when we see ribbons, signs, or blazed trees left to indicate a path. It is always better to discuss the planned route with your group members to avoid the necessity of leaving any markings. Of course, if you must use markers, they should be removed upon your departure.

Cairns, consisting of rocks stacked on top of one another, are commonly used to mark routes through open areas or across rocky outcrops where trail tread disappears. These rock piles are usually located within view of one another, but on occasion may be far enough apart to necessitate a search (see Fig. 4.4). Never remove these markings from official trails.

On occasion, while hiking in the woods you might spot a location poster nailed to a tree. These small posters made of metal and usually painted yellow in color, are sometimes referred to as section markers. They are placed on trees by survey teams representing land management agencies or the U.S. Geological Survey. Many private land-owning companies also install these markers. Inscribed on the poster is the identification of the township, range, and section in which it is located. A diagram shows the quarters contained within the identified

Fig. 4.4. Rock piles or cairns, such as the one shown here, are commonly used to mark routes through open areas or rocky out-crops.

section. Usually a nail hole or inscription along one of the quarter lines is used as the means of identifying the ground location of the poster. Although further explanation is beyond the scope of this book, if you know something about the way townships, ranges, and sections are laid out, there should be little difficulty in identifying your exact ground location on a map.

A thorough discussion of trail orientation requires mention of the fact that paths often vanish when they come to meadows, marshes, rocks, or blowdowns. Much of the time this is because hikers are either allowed to wander on their own through the open space of the meadow or are forced to select their own route around such objects as fallen trees or rocks. Problems arise now and then when a leader has difficulty locating where the trail resumes. When this situation occurs, several members of the group should establish a search pattern, and then fan out to scout for signs of the trail. It is advisable to keep everyone within visual or hearing distance of one another during the search, and a time limit should be established in order for everyone to meet at a designated spot if the trail is not found.

Off-Trail Route Selection

Off-trail or cross-country travel involves yet additional knowledge and skills beyond those already discussed. The pleasures of reaching isolated places in the backcountry without the trail to point the way is often most satisfying. Unfortunately, most people are afraid to get off the beaten track, because they lack the confidence, tools, or imagination to go anywhere they want.

Off-trail hiking involves the use of your map combined with common sense. Once a desired destination has been selected on your map, you must then determine the best route for getting there. Careful study of terrain and elevation changes as noted by map contour lines must next be made. Generally, routes should be selected that have gradual slopes in order to avoid gain or loss in elevation and expenditure of unnecessary energy. A good topographical map will also reveal low saddles and passes you will want to use if passing from one side of a divide to another.

Whether to travel on a valley floor or high on a ridge top is a difficult decision to make by map alone. On-the-ground observation combined with map reading is a   preferable method, but much of the time this is not possible. At any rate, keep in mind that easy travel is more often found on ridge tops than on valley floors, which are frequently plagued with thick vegetation, marsh lands, deadfall, and other hazards. Of course, selection of ridges vs. valleys for travel must also be weighed against each individual situation. For instance, what if there is no snow on the ridge to provide drinking water for your party? Under such circumstances you may be forced to stay near the valley floor, where there is likely to be a spring, stream, or lake.

Terrain viewed from a distance often appears different than when seen close at hand. For instance, the steepness of a mountain slope usually looks great from far away. Yet, when viewing the same slope from a closer vantage point, you likely will not find it as steep and formidable as first thought. Judgment errors in route selection can easily be made unless you are cognizant of this visual phenomenon. There is a continual need to make accurate assessment of potential travel routes from a close distance in addition to comparing what you see with the map.

Also, when selecting off-trail routes, you must know something of the type of ground base that must be traveled, and its related characteristics. Ideal travel is on a hard base with few obstructions, such as when walking on dirt covered with short grass, when traversing a firmly compacted snowfield, or when hiking up a flat slab of rock. Noteworthy are problems created when walking in soft sand, when crossing an expanse of windfall, or when descending a steep mountainside covered with slick bear grass. At times it may be best to take the long route in order to find easy going, and to avoid some of these problems.

Another important aspect related to good cross-country route selection is use of game trails. Our wildlands are literally covered with trails traveled on and made exclusively by animals. These trails are created from frequent use of the same route by large animals, such as deer who wear down the ground cover and level the soil with their hooves. Should we find such a trail going our way, we should certainly take advantage of it. After a long traverse on a steep side slope, it is a great relief to stumble across even a poorly developed animal trail that allows you to flatten your footsteps and equally distribute your weight.

Animals are intelligent in selecting their routes. Like human beings, they also prefer to travel the path of least resistance. In most cases, a game trail provides a good track at a reasonable grade in the direction that it goes. Be careful, however, not to get caught by blindly following a trail no matter where it is headed. If it starts out in your desired direction, but does not continue to do so after a reasonable length of time and distance, then set out on your own. Soon you will likely find yet another trail going your desired direction, provided you move up or down the side of the slope.

In high mountain areas, game trails are most frequently found on south-facing slopes, where the snow is the first to melt in the spring. Also look for trail signs along ridge tops and in saddles and mountain passes. These are good places to find well-worn routes used by animals traveling from one valley to the next.

Like trails made by humans, those made by animals also often disappear in open areas such as meadows. They then resume in the heavy timber where animal grazing and movements are more confined. A little scouting will probably find the continuation of the trail. Also, if a game trail disappears on the side of a slope, you will possibly find it again by scouting up or down for a brief distance. This is common, because grazing wildlife tend to scatter apart as they move up and down the slopes. However, when moving horizontally, they are more likely to follow the same route.

A final word to the wise when traveling off-trail; keep as many different route options open for as long as possible before being forced to close out any of them. This practice allows you to view new and developing circumstances as they occur, and keeps the door open for alteration of plans if desired or needed. It also prevents bullheaded decisions on preplanned routes that can get your party into serious trouble. If necessity arises, do not hesitate to turn around and backtrack in order to get out of a nasty situation. It is much better to admit an error in route determination than to blunder foolishly ahead.

5

HIKING AND CAMPING TECHNIQUES

Low-Impact Camping

For many persons, wildland recreation is a deeply moving experience resulting from close contact with the natural environment. The overall experience is enhanced by the solitude that is normally associated with being away from the city. Consequently, the fewer signs that one sees of people and their impact on the land, the higher the level of the wilderness experience. Our remaining wildlands provide outstanding opportunities for solitude and a primitive and unconfined type of recreation, such as backpacking. However, the primeval character of these undeveloped lands needs to be protected to preserve their natural conditions.

Out of necessity, the old frontier ethic of the pioneers in America was to subdue nature and civilize the wilderness. In earlier years there existed unlimited natural resources, and little worry of their consumption. Camping in those days was a matter of survival and necessity rather than recreation. That same attitude has carried over to far too many modern campers, even though it is no longer appropriate today. We now realize that an adverse human impact in wilderness tends to be immediately and highly conspicuous. Unfortunately, some of the people who visit our wildlands for recreation purposes are actually destroying the very qualities they are seeking. This need not and should not be the case, however.

An inexperienced backpacker may have little awareness of his or her impact on such vulnerable ecological systems as those found in wildlands. The experienced and sophisticated outdoor enthusiasts, on the other hand, have developed an environmental sensitivity that leads to ecologically responsible behavior while in the backcountry. Such persons know that their visit to the wilderness can have an adverse impact on the land, and consequently their personal actions lead to decreased consumption and pollution. In essence, they have adopted the well-established wilderness ethic of low-impact camping, which is based on ecological concerns and attitudes.

The purpose of low-impact camping is to retain the characteristic of nondeveloped beauty, so that all visitors to the backcountry can enjoy this contrast to urban settings. Adopting the wilderness ethic necessitates that we not only come to recognize the fragility of wild areas, but also make a personal commitment to the care and wise use of this environment. Our goal should be to escape detection by leaving the least trace of our presence. To a skilled backpacker, that might mean leaving nothing but bent grass! Signs of aluminum foil, cut boughs, scarred trees, tin cans, soapy water, toilet paper and human waste are simply out of the question. Because of its importance, much of the following discussion in this chapter will emphasize ways of reducing our impact on the land.

Most of the suggestions found here and in other sections of this book are not exacting rules, but rather are practical ideas for reducing our impact on the natural environment and on other people sharing our backcountry areas (see Fig. 5.1). Two leading authorities on this subject aptly point out that those who use minimum-impact camping techniques must be quick to adapt to changing conditions. In their book, *Soft Paths*, Bruce Hampton and David Cole state,

"Visitors must consider the variables of each place—soil, vegetation, wildlife, moisture, the amount and type of use the area receives, and the overall effect of their own use—and then use their judgment to determine which practices to apply (1)."

Camping

In order to allow time to properly establish a campsite, plan to terminate your hike early enough in the day to complete all

COURTESY

Maintain solitude: keep noise to a minimum.

Fig. 5.1. Common courtesies in the backcountry.

If you pack it in, pack it out.

Leave a clean camp.

tasks before evening. It is important that necessary chores be performed—site selected, shelter assembled, water collected, food prepared, meals eaten, utensils washed, and equipment stored—without having to grope around in the dark to do so. Allow adequate time to complete these tasks and to relax before turning in for the night.

Selecting and Setting Up the Campsite

When selecting the actual location of the camp, be aware of such things as convenience of drinking water, natural hazards in the area, and your impact on the land. Of course you must also consider a flat and comfortable location. Research suggests that the least damage to a campsite is caused when you camp on pristine sites that are durable and show no signs of previous use, or on popular high-impacted sites already so heavily damaged that further use will cause little additional deterioration. In contrast, campsites that show obvious signs of prior use, but with a substantial amount of vegetation still surviving, should be avoided altogether (2).

Hence, whenever possible, use an already well-established campsite instead of destroying ground cover in a new location. Try to confine most activities to areas of the site that are already bare. If such an area is unavailable, look for a previously unused spot where your overall impact can be reduced. This can be done by choosing a hard, nonvegetated site on sandy terrain or the forest duff, rather than a site with the lush, delicate, vegetated soil of meadows or stream sides. If you are forced to choose a vegetated site, look for dense patches of dry grass, not an area with fragile low shrubs or succulent plants.

Be considerate of other campers in the area by selecting an individual site. To protect their scenic view, stay away from bodies of water or open meadows and camp well off the trail. Try to camp 200 feet or more from lakes, streams, meadows, and trails when you have a chance. Camping in these areas is also unwise, because you will not only destroy fragile plant communities, but also will be located where the air is cold and damp.

If other parties are close to where you want to camp, move on or choose your campsite so that terrain features ensure privacy. Trees, shrubs, rocks, or small hills will reduce noise substantially. Also, out of respect for nearby campers, keep the noise level low at your campsite.

When camping in pristine places, disperse your activities and use extra care. Space the tents, kitchen, and latrine, and try to avoid concentrating traffic over any area.

Select a smooth, debris-free area on level ground for placing your shelter, if possible. Be sure to consider a location that will catch the early morning sun (if desirable), and avoid potential hazards, such as dead standing trees that could be blown over in a storm. If a campfire is to be built, locate your shelter well away from it, to reduce the possibility of flying sparks burning a hole in your tarp or tent. Trenching around tents is obsolete and should be avoided, so therefore, remember that shelters placed on high spots are naturally dryer and less likely to be a problem than low areas in rain. The best campsites are generally found on ridges, on hills, or near canyon walls, because these areas provide natural drainage. By all means, avoid dry washes or stream banks that could be hit by a flash flood. A further consideration for a safe and comfortable camp is wind. Camps established on the leeward side of ridges, well below mountain passes, are best because they avoid the ventura effect of wind, which increases in velocity as it funnels through such narrow areas.

Once a potential location for a shelter has been found, don't hesitate to actually lie down to try it out. If there is a mild pitch to the landscape, be sure that you can place your head at the higher end. If the site is found suitable, then pitch the shelter over the spot. Be sure to face the tent or tarp opening away from the prevailing wind and secure all ties and stakes properly. Next, prepare your quarters for the night; roll out the ground pad and unpack and fluff your sleeping bag in order to allow time for it to gain maximum loft before bedtime.

At times it may be impossible to locate a flat area or, for that matter, even a mild slope for the shelter. In these rare instances you may be forced to make do with what is available. Sleeping with your head well above your feet is not the most desirable thing to do, because there is a tendency for you to slide downhill. The system can be improved somewhat, however, by placing a "foot log"—a small log or good-sized rock—next to the bottom of the tent or shelter. Such an object provides a sense of security, because it serves as a solid brace for your feet.

Limit your stay to as few nights as possible, to avoid waste accumulation and injury to plants. One night in each campsite is best, and this will make it easier to reduce the impact of your visit when you depart. Before leaving camp, naturalize the area by replacing rocks and scattering leaves and twigs around the site.

Pitching the Tent

Though each tent design has its own unique characteristics, there are some directions that generally apply when setting up most of them. First, select a level, well-drained area for placing the tent, one that is relatively free of debris. A plastic ground cloth is desirable to place under the tent for added protection. Next, unroll the tent, being sure that the entry faces away from the prevailing wind. Using poles and guy lines, erect the head or entrance end of the tent before doing the other end. Then make any final attachments of guy lines so there is even tension on all sides of the tent. If a fly is used, it should fit over the inner tent, but not touch the canopy. Adjustments may be needed from time to time. Remember that a tightly pitched tent will better withstand the forces of wind and water than one that sags.

The normal procedure for anchoring a shelter is to drive stakes into the ground, provided the soil is not too hard or soft. If the soil is too hard or rocky to drive a stake, then it may be necessary to take advantage of nearby shrubs or rocks and tie on to them. On the other hand, anchoring a shelter in snow or sand can present a different dilemma. Here it becomes necessary to tie off guy lines on short sticks, or anything else with a long surface area, and then bury them under the surface as anchors. Simply dig an opening in the snow or sand, place the stick horizontally into the hole, and then cover it completely. Be sure to stamp the sand or snow firmly and, if necessary, pour a small amount of water over the area to allow it to set.

By the way, it is not uncommon for owners of self-standing tents to be lulled into complacency. Such tents should always be anchored securely, even when the wind is calm. An unexpected breeze can roll these shelters like tumbleweeds.

Staying Warm at Night

Here are several suggestions that can help you stay warm in your sleeping bag.

1.   As soon as you set up your shelter, unpack your sleeping bag and fluff it up in order to allow time for it to gain as much loft as possible before use.

2.   Be sure to use a pad under your bag for insulation and comfort.

3.   In order to conserve heat, use a tent or canopy to reduce the chilling effects of wind that can increase conduction away from the surface of the bag.

4.   If you are cold, eat quick-energy food, such as a candy bar, before going to bed. This can improve your heat production ability because more blood sugar is available in the system. Also, physical exercise will increase metabolism. If you are enclosed in your sleeping bag, but are still cold, try isometric exercises, such as pushing your feet or the palms of your hands against each other. Or, try getting undressed inside a close-fitting mummy bag. By the time you are undressed, you will be off to a warm night's sleep. Remember, metabolism is directly related

to production of body heat. Physical condition and amount of rest can affect metabolism.

5.   Keep your bag dry. A wet down sleeping bag can lose all of its warming properties. Synthetics may retain some insulation when wet, but will not be as comfortable as desired. Sometime during the day, either before setting out on the trail in the morning, or after reaching your new campsite, hang up your bag in the sun in order to dry out any dampness caused from body moisture or frost.

Building Campfires

In many backcountry areas, it is best to do without camp-fires altogether unless they are absolutely necessary. Not only do fire scars leave evidence of our presence, but also, due to the small amount of rainfall in some places, wood is a limited resource. The dead and decaying wood is needed by the forests to replace soil nutrients and to provide organic matter. The simple fact is that in many areas, wood is being used faster than it is grown. Therefore, in these places a fire should be considered a luxury to be used only in times of unusual cold or wet conditions, or for very special occasions. A fire certainly is not necessary every evening, particularly if your party is equipped with a small backpacking stove for cooking meals. Those who use a stove rather than a campfire benefit by the simplicity and freedom of not having to gather kindling, breathe smoke, or extinguish and disguise the fire ring before moving on. Likewise, they find that they are not isolated from the night and the larger world that would otherwise be obscured by the flickering fire.

If you do choose to have a fire, it is best to do so in an area where one has been built before, instead of creating yet an additional fire ring or scar in a new location. Elaborate fireplaces are unnecessary, as are large bonfires. Keep your fire small, allowing people to gather closely around it. Also, have fires only in areas with plentiful wood and rapid resource replenishment. For example, to cause less impact, use firewood from a thick stand of lodgepole pines, not from trees near the timberline.

Don't build a fire on the forest floor, as duff is easily ignited and can spread to other areas. Choose a spot away from over-hanging branches, tree roots, or rock ledges. Despite the fact that overhanging rocks can serve to reflect heat, such places should not be used for fires, because smoke will leave a permanent black mark. Should there be no opportunity to build a fire in an already existing fire circle, then look for a spot along the edge of a stream or river that might have a sand beach. If a sandy location is not available, then build the campfire either in a pit dug into the ground (pit fire method), or on a mound of mineral soil spread over a flat rock (flat rock/mound fire method).

To build a pit fire, select a place void of vegetation with exposed mineral or sandy soil. Carefully scrape away any ground cover of duff and litter until you are down to mineral soil. Be sure you are down below the humus layer, and then continue digging or scraping a shallow hole several inches into the mineral soil in order to create a base for the fire. Be certain you have scraped away all of the humus because humus soil can smolder and burn under the surface of the ground, and later surface and ignite elsewhere to cause a forest fire. Your fire pit is now ready for use. Please avoid the age-old tradition of encircling the fire pit with rocks, for they will be scarred black, leaving a permanent sign of your temporary stay.

Prior to vacating the campsite, you should eradicate all traces of fire. Be sure all charred wood has been burned completely and that the fire is so thoroughly out that it is cold to the touch—including the ground underneath the fire area. Also, be certain that there are no smoldering roots or humus. The remaining gray soot and black coals can then be crushed and dispersed widely in the least conspicuous manner possible. Finally, replace the ground cover and camouflage the site with mineral soil, pine needles, or other natural litter materials that match the surroundings.

In the recent past, it was the practice of various hiking groups, including the National Outdoor Leadership School (NOLS), to build pit fires even in areas covered with grass and other lush vegetation. The conventional procedure for preparing the fire pit was to remove the surface vegetation intact and carefully set it aside from the fire site. When the fire was completely burned out, the original vegetation was then replaced exactly as it had been removed. To aid in recovery of the grass, water was also carried to and sprinkled on the site. Although this practice seemed to make sense, it unfortunately did not prove to be entirely satisfactory. Hampton and Cole report that NOLS personnel investigated many of these kinds of campfire sites after use, and discovered not only damaged vegetation surrounding the site, but also sunken depressions where the pits themselves had been dug (3). Moreover, animals had often excavated the old fire pits. Consequently, where ground vegetation will most likely be damaged, a flat rock/mound fire seems a better choice.

For the flat rock/mound fire method, spread at least three inches of carefully gathered bare soil on top of one or more flat rocks, being sure this layer of insulating mineral soil covers an area slightly larger than the fire will occupy. Next, build your fire as usual. Burn all wood completely, and after the fire is out, crush and scatter any coals. After the soil is removed and the rock rinsed, the area will be virtually unscarred.

The skills necessary for fire building are improved over time by practice. When preparing for the fire itself, first collect all necessary tinder and kindling, making sure that there is sufficient wood so you will not need to seek additional fuel after dark. Select firewood first from loose branches and sticks on the ground, and next from downed trees; avoid taking limbs and branches from standing dead trees, as they are a part of the beauty of the backcountry. Of course, living trees should also be left alone.

Tinder in the form of dry pine needles, small twigs, and dead grass, etc., is used for igniting the larger pieces of kindling wood. Starting with a compact wad of tinder in the middle, arrange the kindling closely around it, beginning with smaller sticks; once the fire begins to take hold and burn well, you can then add larger ones.

The fire is lighted only when everything else is ready and should never be left unattended once started. Igniting the fire, however, is not always as easy as it might seem, particularly if there is damp wood or a breeze. To assist in getting the tinder to burn, small pieces of dry pitch can often be found on the trunk or branches of pine trees. This substance is volatile enough that only a few small pieces added to the tinder will assure a good fire start. Some campers simply pour a small amount of white gas over the wood to assist ignition, but this is potentially dangerous and is normally not recommended. A much safer alternative is to carry a small amount of commercially-made fire starter, which is available from most outdoor shops. Another alternative is to carry a small container of charcoal starting fluid. A candle is also a useful device when starting fires.

Using Proper Sanitation

Disposal of waste and refuse in the backcountry is most important; improper care of such matter can result in pollution, contamination, and unsightliness. Proper handling of sanitation will leave the land clean and attractive for you and others to enjoy.

Most campsites used by backpackers do not have even the most basic sanitation facilities. There are no garbage collections and no toilets. You have to manage without these conveniences; but how do you do this? There are right and wrong ways of disposing of wastes in the backcountry. The proven methods of such waste disposal follow.

Human Waste

Hampton and Cole point out that solid body waste disposal in the backcountry should be dealt with in such a way as to minimize the chance of water pollution, minimize the chance of anything or anyone finding the waste, and maximize the rate of decomposition (4). This is good advice.

Fortunately, human waste is biodegradable and will return to nature. There has been a common belief that the process is speeded up when human waste is mixed with bacteria located in the top four to ten inches of soil. At these depths, the system of biological decomposers supposedly works quickly to dispose of organic material. Unfortunately, at least one study refutes this theory (5). Nonetheless, even if buried human waste decomposes slower than when left at the ground surface, the "cat method" typically remains the technique of choice. If for no other reason, it decreases the likelihood that human feces will come in contact with sources of water, insects, or other humans.

The "cat method" includes the following steps: Select a suitable screened spot at least 200 feet from any open water and well away from any trail. (Groups may need to walk over 200 feet to assure cat holes are scattered during their stay at that site.)

Either with the heel of the boot or with a small digging tool (a light garden trowel is good), make a small hole, taking care to dig down into the humus layer. Keep the sod intact if possible. After use, simply fill the hole with the loose dirt and then lightly tramp in the sod. Nature will do the rest.

If you are up to it, use leaves, snow, and other natural substitutes in preference to toilet paper. If you do use toilet paper, burn it up completely if possible. Try locating yourself in a safe area away from combustible fuels, and be extremely wary of spreading fire. By all means, make sure the fire is completely out when you are done. If fire danger is high, simply pack the used toilet paper in a plastic bag and either carry it out or burn it later in a campfire. Tampons should not be buried because animals dig them up. Either burn them in an extremely hot fire or, if you are not in Grizzly bear country, bag and pack them out.

Though it does not require the cat method, urination should be done well away from trails and water sources. Try to avoid vegetation because the acidity of urine can affect plant growth.

To prevent sanitation problems from extremely heavy visitation in the backcountry, latrines may be warranted in certain situations—such as for extended campsite use by large groups at popular sites in the wilderness. We simply have to consider all the benefits and detriments of concentrating all human waste in one spot, vs. having each individual select his or her own area. If the decision is to have a latrine, locate it on high ground at least 200 feet from any stream, lake, or marshy area so the human waste will be filtered through the soil. Make the hole wider than it is deep, but preferably have at least a foot in depth to minimize animal excavation. If the latrine is located in an appropriate area away from combustible fuels, then burn toilet paper in the trench, but do so only if you can avoid starting fires around the latrine. Keep the spade handy for spreading a layer of dirt over the latrine after each use, and fill in the hole once it is within four inches of being full. Before leaving the campsite, be sure to replace all of the sod and naturalize the area.

Trash

Cans, bottles, aluminum foil, and anything else that will not burn should be carried out of the backcountry. Bring along a plastic garbage bag for this purpose. Burying is not satisfactory because the material is often exposed later by animals or frost action.

If you have a campfire, burn all paper and other burnable material. Be careful, though, not to include aluminum foil wrappings or packages, such as those used for freeze-dried foods, instant hot chocolate, or soups. Most campfires do not reach appropriate temperatures to burn these foils completely; what remains is difficult to sort from the ashes.

Nothing should be left behind. Although certain food scraps, such as egg and peanut shells and orange peels, are biodegradable, they still take a very long time to decompose and create a visual pollution for other hikers. Any leftover food scraps that cannot be burned completely should be carried out in plastic bags.

Fish intestines should be burned completely in a campfire. However, if there are scavenger animals and birds around, if there are not many remains, and if the area is lightly used, then the intestines can be scattered in discreet and far away places to decompose naturally. Use your best judgment.

Washing

Personal bathing or washing of cooking utensils or clothing should not be done directly in any body of water—even with biodegradable detergent. Any soap, biodegradable or not, causes pollution to streams, ponds, or lakes. To clean dishes, clothing, or yourself, carry water up on the shore, and well away from the water supply as far as is practical. The recommended minimum distance is at least 50 feet. This allows your soap water to drain on vegetation-covered soil that can filter out the soap and break it down.

For washing dishes or bathing, a polyethylene ground sheet can often come in handy. To use it, find a dip or low spot on the ground, cover it with the plastic sheet, and fill with water.

Loading and Wearing the Backpack

Carrying a backpack should not be a test of physical endurance; instead, it should allow you freedom and independence to walk where you want to go and enjoy the country. Unfortunately, there are so many variables to consider that no one has yet been able to   prescribe accurately the maximum amount of weight an individual should carry for efficiency and enjoyment. On the other hand, there have been attempts to establish some rough guidelines. One common rule in determining the heaviest load to carry is to take no more than one-third of your body weight if you are in good condition, and no more than one-fourth if you are out of shape. Keep in mind that this formula applies to maximum weight, which would be far more than needed on most trips. In fact, there is no reason to carry such a burden unless you either must take along all of your drinking water or are planning an extended expedition beyond three weeks' duration. A more ideal pack weight, allowing for comfort and agility in the backcountry, is no more than one-fifth of your own body weight. So much the better if you can cut the weight even further, and still take along everything you need. Keep in mind that the amount of enjoyment gained from a wilderness trip is often in reverse proportion to the total amount of unnecessary weight carried.

Loading for Comfort

In addition to total weight, how the pack is loaded can affect your comfort. Many experienced persons find that the heavy objects should be placed near the top of the bag, and close to your back. This aligns the heavy items more closely with your center of gravity, while keeping the pack from pulling back on the shoulders. Packs constructed with separate horizontal compartments have the advantage of allowing you to control more easily this type of weight distribution. Also, be sure to place often-needed items, such as snacks or rain gear, in a readily accessible location. As for the sleeping bag, it is stored in a stuff sack and then placed inside and near the bottom of an internal frame pack bag, or in the case of an external frame pack, it is attached with straps to the outside lower back frame. On the other hand, if you happen to have a full-length external frame pack that extends to the bottom of the frame, then the sleeping bag must be stored inside.

For the sake of convenience, know where each item is stored in your backpack. Try using varying sizes of nylon or plastic stuff sacks for holding things like clothing and toilet articles. These sacks are also handy for separately bagging food items according to when they will be eaten. Label each bag for quick and easy identification. This prevents the need for opening each bag when looking for a specific item. Finally, each time you load your backpack, make a habit of placing each item in the same location. This saves time when attempting to find an article in the dark of night, or in case of an emergency.

Use waterproof stuff sacks to keep things dry inside the pack during inclement weather. Plastic garbage bags are suitable for this, but they tend to rip easily. Try placing them inside a nylon bag, which can serve as a reinforcing shell. An additional way of keeping things dry is to purchase or make a waterproof nylon rain cover that fits over the outside of the entire backpack (see Fig. 5.2). A large plastic garbage bag, although not as durable, also provides a good shelter for the pack.

Fig. 5.2. Waterproof nylon rain cover over the pack.

Wearing the Pack

Both internal and external frame backpacks are modern engineering marvels designed to distribute the weight so that most of it rests on the hips rather than on the neck and shoulders. A pack should ride steady and lightly, with its weight carried mostly by hips and legs. To do this, however, you must be sure to take advantage of the waist strap, which is attached to the lower end of the frame. First, place the pack on your back, and tighten the shoulder straps until the pack is held comfortably against the back. Next, hunch up the shoulders and fasten the buckle of the waist belt. The waist belt should then be cinched tightly in order to hold the weight of the pack directly on the hips once the hunched shoulders are lowered. With the weight now on the hips, the shoulders primarily lend stability to the pack by holding it in a vertical position against the back. With only minor and infrequent adjustments, this technique should allow you to walk many miles without feeling undue strain on any part of the body.

For proper pack comfort, be sure that the waist belt and shoulder straps fit right. The hip belt should rest on your hip-bones with the padded section of the belt wrapped around your hips, but not quite meeting in the front. You may have to move the belt up or down on an external frame pack, so the lower crossbar does not contact your lower back (see Fig. 5.3).

With most packs, shoulder-strap upper anchor points should be even with the crest of your shoulders, and the straps should be set wide enough not to pinch your neck. If the straps are mounted too high, they transfer weight to the front of your shoulders; if set too low, they take too much of the load and don't allow the waist belt to share the burden.

Some shoulder straps are equipped with load-lifters, which stabilize the upper part of the pack and take the load off the top of your shoulders. The load-lifters generally should join the shoulder straps just forward of the shoulder crest, and join the pack frame at roughly ear level. Tighten them to transfer more weight onto your shoulders, or loosen them to settle the weight onto the hips. Many shoulder straps also come equipped with a sternum strap. This feature, which should be adjustable up and down, keeps the shoulder straps from sliding out and riding on the points of your shoulders.

Fig. 5.3. For proper pack comfort, be sure the shoulder straps, hip belt, load-lifter straps, sternum strap, and all other belts are adjusted properly.

Hiking

There are a number of things that can be done to improve our hiking technique, whether we're walking on a trail or traveling cross-country. Still, we must continually be reminded of our impact on the land and ways of reducing it.

Walking

It is common to see some hikers tie such items as cups, water bottles, and clothing onto the outside of their packs and head down the trail. Although such items are readily accessible, this is not a good practice, because all equipment should be packed inside the backpack so nothing will be lost or snagged on a bush or limb. Generally good practice will also keep the weight of the pack centered over your back, so there is less likelihood of your being thrown off balance.

Preparation

Before hoisting your pack and starting out, make proper clothing adjustments, for a change in body temperature can soon be expected. If your temperature is suitable before you begin, then expect the exercise from walking to warm you beyond a comfortable level. For best results, adjust your clothing before beginning by starting a little on the cool side. Within a few minutes you will probably feel just fine. By following this practice, you will eliminate the need to stop for a clothing adjustment shortly after starting your hike. However, should additional clothing adjustments be needed from time to time, be sure to make them before becoming too hot or cold.

Pace and Stride

A group's walking speed should be the same at the end of the day as it is at the beginning. From the outset, plan your pace accordingly, keeping in mind that a long day's hike lies ahead. Your speed should be one that everyone in the party can maintain over a sustained period of time. A common mistake is to start out too fast. Since the gait should be comfortable for the slowest member of the party, it is sometimes advisable to place the slowpoke at the front of the line.

Early in the hike, rhythm in pace and stride is important to establish. The stride should be smooth and easy, assisted by a natural but slight forward lean of the body, and a rhythmic swing of the arms. While walking on flat ground, the length and tempo of the step should be consistent. That same tempo and unbroken rhythm should also be maintained, even when going uphill or downhill, although the length of the stride will change. While going up steep grades, the stride should be shorter, and while going down it should be longer—but the tempo and rhythm should be the same.

As individuals have their own rhythms and differences in length of stride, don't get in the habit of trying to match that of the person in front of you. To avoid this, maintain a suitable distance between others in your group, by spacing at least 10 to 15 feet between one another. By doing this, there is also less likelihood of being hit in the face by a branch or bush that might catch on the person in front.

In order to save energy and maintain a constant pace, don't climb anything you don't have to—even if it is only a 6-inch-high rock or a fallen log. The rule of the game is to step over, not on, the obstacle. Over time, the added energy used to lift the body even a short distance is much greater than simply lifting the leg over or around the obstacle.

Breath Control

Proper breath control, once learned, is yet another important ingredient for maintaining endurance and energy output. Again, each individual must discover his or her own breathing pace, but the important point is to maintain consistency in rhythm.

One way of establishing a rhythmic breathing pattern is to count the number of footsteps taken while either inhaling or exhaling. Some persons, for example, will find that they can comfortably take three steps while breathing in or out. If this pace is appropriate, then attempt to maintain that breathing pattern throughout the hike. This will take a little conscious effort at first, but soon it becomes quite natural.

Try to establish a hiking speed that allows you to have a controlled, rhythmic breathing rate that keeps the heartbeat even. Be alert to monitor your body for any change in heart rate or breath. Doing so will also establish a consistent amount of body heat output, and will eliminate the need to remove or add clothing, as long as the outside temperature remains the same.

The Rest Step

As already mentioned, the length of your stride should shorten when going up steep inclines; the steeper the hill, the shorter the stride. This allows your weight to remain centered over the feet, and relieves some of the strain on leg muscles. However, on extremely steep slopes, there is an additional system of walking, referred to as the rest step or locked knee step, which can further ease the strain of the climb.

The rest step technique is easy to learn; once mastered, steep inclines can be conquered with ease. As you take each step, rock your weight forward onto the front leg; then straighten it completely, locking the weight-bearing knee; then pause for a split-second while resting that leg. This allows the bone structure to bear your weight while giving the leg muscles a moment's rest between each step. With each additional step, shift your weight as described and rest as you rock forward. It is convenient to practice this step on stairways before hitting the trail.

When carrying heavy loads or attacking extreme slopes, it may be necessary to shorten the length of the stride so that one foot is extended forward only inches in front of the other before locking the knee. You can walk this way quickly or slowly, with a minimum of fatigue.

Taking Rest Stops

Once the proper hiking tempo is set, it can be maintained over long periods of time without frequent stops along the trail. Nevertheless, because of the body's constant energy output as well as the extra weight on your back, there is still a need to plan short "breathers" or pack breaks throughout the day. These brief stops should be scheduled between 30 and 60 minutes apart, depending on the physical condition of the group, and the nature of the terrain hiked. Each stop should be short, lasting perhaps only two or three minutes before moving on. Avoid the temptation to stretch the breaks for longer periods of time, because doing so allows body temperatures to cool and muscles to stiffen. It is much easier to get started and to regain the hiking rhythm if this is not allowed to happen. Of course, a longer period of rest should be allowed during the lunch break.

A short, but very relaxing and restful trail break may not necessitate that you remove the backpack and then sit down. Some experienced hikers find it convenient to simply take a standing rest stop. This is correctly done by first releasing the waist belt and then, with the feet spread to shoulders' width, simultaneously bending at the knees and waist until the back is parallel with the ground. The hands are placed on the knees with the elbows locked. By doing this, the strain on the shoulders is relieved because the weight of the pack is shifted to the arms and knees.

Cross-Country Traveling

Cross-country travel is much different than walking on a trail, and requires that you have practice and experience to be proficient. At the same time, application of a little common sense will usually get you where you want to go without too much difficulty. Nevertheless, the trail no longer points the way, so you must analyze the terrain to interpret through the lay of the land precisely where you would like to go (see "Off-Trail Route Selection" in Chapter 4); a few basic hiking techniques are then applied to get you there.

Walk the Contour

The hiking pace for cross-country travel is slow, because constant attention must be given to placing the feet on broken or uneven ground, while continually surveying the route ahead. To gain distance when walking on a slope, follow the old adage of preserving elevation or altitude. In other words, never lose or gain elevation unnecessarily. This can be accomplished by following the imaginary contour of a side hill.

Traverse Routes

When going up or down steep faces, frequently scan the terrain a dozen yards in front in order to pick the easiest going, but continue to watch where you put your feet. A traverse route or zig-zag course is better to follow than a straight attack. By continually switching back and forth, you will be hiking more gradually, and this will be easier on the legs, because the lift is reduced over a longer period of time and distance. This method allows for better footing, and switches the stress from one leg to the other at each turn.

With properly soled boots, you can walk up very steep slopes relying on friction alone. Body weight should be balanced over the feet to keep the weight on the soles. Avoid the natural tendency to lean into the slope, because this reduces boot friction and generates an undesirable outward force of the foot.

Three-Point Support

On extremely steep faces it may be impossible to maintain a body-upright position. Even so, you can continue to move upward by using the rock scrambling technique to ensure a safe footing or hold. This requires that you maintain three points of contact at all times. These contact points can be either both feet and one handhold, or both hands and one foot. The remaining hand or foot is then free to reach for the next hold or step. By allowing only one limb to move at a time, you will still have two secure points of support even if the third one gives way.

Always test each hold or step to see that it is secure before using it. Also, bear most of the weight of the body with the legs, and lean away from the pitch by standing erect, because this keeps the weight over the feet.

Never attempt to climb hazardous ledges or slopes that potentially could cause injuries in a fall. Such areas should be tackled only by experienced mountaineers equipped with ropes and other climbing gear.

Choose the Route Well

Before starting into an untrailed area, you should make a visual survey of the terrain by viewing it from some suitable vantage point. The map will also assist you in selecting a route free of major obstacles. Keep in mind that brush can make progress difficult and tiresome. In the spring, travel is often easier on rocks or on snow that covers the brush. Also, be on the lookout for grassy meadows or slopes; otherwise, follow ridges that are usually bare.

Mountain soils are very fragile and subject to damage, particularly in the spring. Consider that lug-soled boots can tear and break open the tundra surface. A group of hikers tramping in a row can cause irreparable damage to delicate plant life, and create channels for erosion in the soil. Therefore, for traveling across country without trails, especially in tundra or meadows, a group should fan out, rather than walk one behind the other. For the same reason, smooth-soled boots or running shoes are often recommended for tundra hiking whenever practical. By all means, avoid areas that are delicate, such as wet soils or steep and unstable slopes.

Crossing Waterways

Fording rivers or streams can present a problem if there are no fallen logs or exposed rocks to form a natural bridge. Still, if the current is not too strong nor the water too deep, you may choose to wade across. However, some waterways that are easily waded in the summer may actually be impassable in the spring, during the season of melting snow and high run-off.

Before attempting to wade a stream, look for a wide spot where the water depth is shallow. For better balance, find yourself a long, sturdy stick to serve as a walking staff during the crossing. Also, in case of a slip, it is a good idea to undo the waist belt to your pack. Avoid wading in bare feet; a pair of running shoes or camp boots can be worn. If these are not available, you may be forced to wear your hiking boots instead. In either case, remove your socks to keep them dry and, once on the other side, put them back on. Even though the boots may be soaked, the socks will still keep the feet dry and warm.

If the water is too deep to wade safely without assistance, then the use of a rope may be required. At no time, however, should anyone in the water ever be tied to the rope. The first person to make the crossing should simply hold onto the rope, while being belayed from upstream by another member of the party. When traversing the waterway, move at an angle with the current. Better balance and footing can be maintained in heavy rapids by facing upstream and moving sideways while leaning against the current.

Once the first person reaches the opposite bank, the belay line should be tied off at both ends on trees or other sturdy objects so others can use the rope as a hand line. The last person to come across is belayed in the same manner as previously described.

Under no circumstances should a crossing be attempted if the water creates too great a hazard. In the high country, it is not uncommon to face this situation during spring run-offs or following a heavy rain. By checking upstream, however, often a safe crossing can be located above the tributary or where smaller forks join the main water course. If not, you would be wise to abandon your hike or alter the original destination.

Etiquette

Thus far you have learned to overcome some technical difficulties so you can safely enjoy the wildlands, and you have learned some of the ways of being responsible to the natural environment. Still, the discussion on hiking and camping techniques would not be complete without a look at the subject of backcountry etiquette. In the wilderness, as everywhere, there are common courtesies that should be extended not only to others, but to Mother Nature.

For the moment, let's focus on what can be done to reduce our impact on other backcountry users in the area. For instance, our travel should be quiet; noise pollution affects the enjoyment of hikers by reducing the feeling of solitude and lessens the chance of seeing wildlife. One thing we can do is avoid tying cups or cook pots on the outside of our backpacks, because they might bounce and clang as we walk. Likewise, except when absolutely necessary, we should abstain from yelling or whistling, so our sounds are in peaceful harmony. Limiting group size will also minimize noise and visual impact and will reduce wear on the land. We can plan on traveling and camping with fewer than eight people, and they can be divided into hiking groups of two to four during the day. In addition, it is easier to plan for small groups, and easier to keep them together. Campsites for smaller groups are quicker to find, and these campsites harmonize better with the environment.

When meeting other parties on the trail, good manners dictate the following: Hikers coming downhill have the right of way; the party coming uphill should step aside and let them pass. If a group heading in your direction catches you, you as the slower party should let them pass. Groups mounted on horses or supported by stock should be given access to the trail. Horses and mules have individual temperaments and moods, and they can be very unpredictable. Consequently, your unexpected appearance, sudden movement, or loud voice can put these animals on alert, and perhaps cause them to panic and bolt. The problem can be intensified when encountering a string of pack animals or a group of inexperienced horseback riders. The effect could be serious, as each animal successively reacts to the fear of the adjacent one. In the worst case, the animals could dump their riders or gear, break tack, hurt people or themselves, and run away, leaving the horseless riders with a lot of work—not to mention a lasting prejudice against campers on foot.

So how do you, the conscientious hiker, deal with confrontations with stock? Here are some guidelines: Your party, staying in full view of the horses, should immediately get to the downhill side of the trail, stand still, and wait for them to pass. If possible, stand at least 15 feet away, and in a soft but courteous voice, exchange greetings with the oncoming group. This will tend to calm the stock, which are easily spooked, especially by persons wearing brightly-colored backpacks. Watch for signs that the animals are nervous, and be prepared to move if necessary. Warning signs that a horse or mule exhibits when anxious or excited can be any of the following: ears lying back, tail swishing hard or being held tightly to buttocks, body being tense, dancing around or rearing, feet rapidly pawing the ground, teeth chomping the bit, head being thrown around, eyes rolling, or nose loudly snorting. You should move slowly back on the trail only after the string has completely passed you and is well down the trail.

In some areas you may find fences and gates across the trail. On public lands, these are constructed to control the movement of domestic animals that might be grazing. As a common courtesy, leave any gate as you find it, whether open or closed.

Finally, let us now turn our attention to a few additional things that can be done to reduce our impact on the land. First, do not cut corners on the trail. Trail switch-backs, when built and maintained by land managers, are graded to prevent erosion. It is not uncommon along more heavily-used trails to encounter evidence where overzealous hikers have taken shortcuts across steep terrain rather than staying on designated switch-back routes. The result of such maneuvers tends to leave badly eroded areas where the once enjoyable vegetation that held the soil in place has been trampled and killed. Whole sections of a trail can be washed away by the gullies formed. To further retard trail deterioration, groups of hikers should walk single file in the center of the path; this will avoid widening the path or creating multiple lanes.

Many trails have been marked by resource managers with signs that are helpful in determining directions. Likewise, where a trail is less visible, small piles of rocks are often stacked at regular intervals to tell the way. These small cairns show the easiest route across the land. Take care to leave these signs where they are, because such markings, if left intact, may prevent the next group from facing discomfort or danger that can accompany trailblazing.

A few other points should be mentioned with respect to courtesies and responsibilities in the wilds. For instance, to maintain a clean landscape beside the trail, it is good to pick up any litter along the route; have one pocket of your pack available for trash, or carry a plastic litter bag for the refuse. Furthermore, if there are any cigarette smokers in the group, they should never light up while walking, but instead should sit down in a clearing where there is less likelihood of starting a fire. When done, a smoker should "field dress" the cigarette to be sure it is completely out and place the filter and any excess paper in the pocket or the litter bag. Finally, we all should avoid the picking of wildflowers, because they should be left in their natural state for others to see.

If the previously mentioned backcountry manners are respected and accepted as common courtesies by today's users, many future recreationists will be able to enjoy the same routes to rewarding destinations.

1.Hampton, Bruce and David Cole, *Soft Paths*, Stackpole Books, 1988, p. 16
2. Ibid., p. 35-46.
3. Ibid., p. 56.
4. Ibid., p. 67
5. Ibid., p. 68

6

SAFETY AND SURVIVAL

Backpacking is a relatively safe recreational pursuit in terms of the number and severity of accidents and injuries that occur. However, even when minor accidents do take place in the wilds, they can present serious problems, because treatment cannot always be carried out in a normal, routine manner. It is for this reason that a basic understanding of accident prevention, common hazards, and emergency procedures is necessary prior to venturing forth in the backcountry.

The popular connotation of wilderness survival is the ability to live (survive) off the land should situations dictate the necessity to do so. We commonly think of survival techniques as building shelters out of natural materials, building fires, collecting and eating natural foods, and constructing tools and equipment by hand. In other words, the emphasis is often on what to do after one gets into trouble, rather than how to keep from getting into trouble in the first place. Although these survival skills might come in handy under dire emergency situations, it seems appropriate to consider first those things that can prevent us from ever being placed in a survival situation.

Safety Aspects

Proper planning, experience, and common sense create the basic backbone for a pleasant, but safe backcountry experience.

The following discussion covers some of the basic considerations for a backpacking trip.

Be Physically Fit

Because backpacking is a physical activity, a certain degree of physical fitness is necessary in order to participate properly. Good fitness is beneficial because we are more inclined to enjoy hiking and less likely to become fatigued at the end of the day, when accidents are more apt to occur. It is a known fact that a high percentage of backpacking accidents take place late in the day. We should be aware that fatigue affects not only the occurrence of accidents, but also our ability to deal with such crisis situations when they do take place. A fatigued individual has a reduced ability to make sound decisions and to act under stress.

One of the best conditioning exercises for backpackers is running long distances. The development of strong legs and good aerobic capacity results from scheduled runs of at least two miles in length. Running should be done consistently for a minimum of four days a week and should begin well in advance (two months or more) of the backpack season. Of course, cross-training is always good, including a mixture or rotation of distance walking, jogging, cycling, and other aerobic activities.

Know the Weather

A wide assortment of problems in the backcountry can be directly or indirectly related to weather. Unpredicted hot or cold temperatures, as well as unexpected rain, snow, wind, or lightning can create hazardous situations if people are not prepared to deal with such extremes. Proper weather information should always be sought prior to trip departure. Read the weather reports in the local newspaper, call the weather bureau for the most up-to-date predictions, and tune in the radio for any last-minute changes before setting forth at the trailhead.

Although you hope for the best weather, you should plan for the worst. Adequate clothing and shelter for moisture protection and warmth should accompany every trip, even if you are fairly certain that such equipment will not be needed. Should the weather reports indicate unfavorable conditions for an outing, be prepared for postponement or alternative plans. Once you become experienced and adequately equipped with proper supplies and clothing, there should be few times when cancellation will be necessary.

Become Familiar with the Area

At least one member of every backpacking group should be informed or familiar with the travel area to be visited. Knowledge of an area can usually be gained by reading guidebooks and maps, visiting with area resource managers, and/or talking with others who have previously visited the area. The party leader should have a good understanding of (1) the nature and difficulty of the terrain, (2) access to alternative exits from the backcountry in case of emergencies, (3) the condition of trails if they exist, (4) potential water supply sites, and (5) vehicle access routes to the trailhead and trailend. This final point should not be taken lightly, because in some instances it is more difficult to locate the trailhead than to find one's way through the backcountry.

Tell Someone You Are Going

Emergencies can be created and amplified simply because people leave on extended trips and forget to tell anyone. Always inform at least one responsible person of the location of your trip, the number of people in the party, and the estimated trip schedule, including the approximate time of return. Should problems prevent you from returning home on schedule, you can be reasonably sure that proper authorities will be notified, and little time or energy will be lost locating your group. In far too many cases, failure to follow these simple procedures results in a loss of valuable time in initiating a search, endangers the lives of search parties, and wastes many hours and dollars associated with the use of expensive equipment for search and rescue operations.

Plan for Delays

An experienced backpacker plans for delays because there are a number of reasons a group may not always be able to meet a scheduled agenda. When time is not allowed for an unexpected delay, then the party must act under pressure to make up for the subsequent loss. Decisions made under this pressure can often be wrong, and lead to further confusion or panic at a time when a cool head is needed. Emergency situations may be compounded when important decisions are influenced by the "homing instinct"—the feeling of a need or obligation to be home by a certain time or date. In summary, try not to obligate yourself to be home for dinner at 6:00 or to be back the night before your wedding. Forego the trip if there is any potential chance you will miss an important appointment or obligation.

Sign Out with Local Authorities

Many of the land-managing agencies desire that users register with them prior to entering the backcountry. In fact, in some of the more popular, heavily-used wilderness areas, use permits must be obtained before hiking or camping. Whether required or not, it is good practice to let the managing agency know of your plans prior to the start of the trip. They should be informed also of the successful completion of the journey.

Keep the Party Together

Any time two or more persons travel together in the backcountry, there likely will be differences in hiking speeds as well as the desired time between rest stops along the trail. For these and other reasons, it is quite easy for individual members of a party to become spread out along the route and to lose track of one another. The temptation to go one's own way in hopes of later catching up or finding the group is a bad practice that can lead to complete separation of the party. The best procedure is for the total group to stay together at all times. It is reasonable to expect some distance to develop between those with fast and slow hiking paces, but some compromises must be made on the part of the faster members of the group in order to stay within proximity of the total party.

Often it is helpful to place the slower hikers at the front of the group. This not only keeps the faster hikers from getting too far ahead, but also seems to assist in improving the hiking pace of the slower members of the party. There evidently is a psychological advantage to being at the front of the line.

Call Short Rest Stops

Short rest stops along the trail should be taken periodically. These rest periods should be brief, lasting perhaps no longer than three or four minutes, because muscles tend to stiffen quickly. The body can also become chilled during longer breaks. Hiking groups tend to discover that the desired amount of time between stops usually ranges from thirty to fifty minutes, depending upon the group speed and the physical condition of individual members of the party. These rest periods, although brief, are nonetheless valuable adjustment periods that enable the human body to sustain a consistent workload throughout the entire day.

Stop Early in the Day

Daily hiking schedules should call for early stops, which allow adequate time to establish a comfortable camp and prepare a good meal. In far too many cases, backpackers continue to hike well into the late afternoon and evening. They arrive at their destination in the dark, exhausted, and too tired to care properly for their personal needs. During ideal conditions, such practices may lead to no further complications; on the other hand, problems such as deteriorating weather or injuries can add enough additional burden to be serious. Proper planning should allow for a selection of alternative campsites to be used in case the original location cannot be reached as early as planned.

Be Prepared to Cope with the Unexpected

Even the best of plans can go astray, so one should be prepared to cope with the unexpected. The outing organizer should anticipate and plan for emergencies such as accidents or getting lost. The party should know (1) whom to notify first in case of an accident; (2) who will take charge if the leader is injured; (3) who can accompany an ill or injured hiker out of the backcountry; (4) who is responsible for hospital, doctor, and rescue bills; and (5) what to do if the group becomes separated. Study your map to know where to go for help if needed. Where is the nearest ranger station or roadhead—and what is the best route to get there?

If you find yourself in a situation where you are lost or

stranded, the natural reaction is panic. In order to overcome this fear, it is often helpful to sit down and think back over past events to see if you can retrace your footsteps or travel pattern. If you realize you will be unable to return to your camp destination or are uncertain as to your location, commit yourself to spending the night where you are. With adequate time to prepare for the night, you should be able to develop a good shelter and make yourself reasonably comfortable. Pick the best campsite in the immediate area and build a small fire if needed. Campsite selection should include readily available firewood, materials for shelter construction, and freedom from natural hazards. Availability of drinking water is another important factor. If you do not have materials with you for construction of a shelter, build a lean-to or fashion a shelter from available natural materials. It should be understood, however, that only under emergency situations would such a practice be tolerated according to today's environmental standards. Use of live trees or boughs is not recommended for ordinary camping, because of the unnecessary destruction of foliage.

If you find yourself in a survival situation, there are five things you should consider: (1) prevention of, or care of, physical injury; (2) protection from the elements; (3) acquisition of water and food; (4) prevention of exhaustion and/or hypothermia (exposure); and (5) preparation for rescue. Your best survival tool is your head—use it! Do only what is necessary after thinking it out. Remember, if you have informed others of where you are backpacking and they also know when you are to be home, then it will be only a matter of time before you will be missed and a search will be organized.

Natural Hazards

Backpackers are constantly confronted by a wide variety of natural hazards associated with weather, terrain, and wildlife. In this section, some of the more common problems are discussed.

Weather Problems

Earlier in this chapter we discussed the importance of knowing what weather might be expected while on a backpacking trip and how to go about learning of weather predictions. From time to time, however, we are apt to confront Mother Nature at her worst. Therefore, knowing how to deal with the elements is basic to backpacking.

Unseasonable cold weather can present little difficulty to the prepared outdoor enthusiast. Always be prepared to dress by using the layer system, so that a constant envelope of comfortable, still air remains around your body at all times. The layer system involves wearing a number of different garments, one on top of the next, rather than one heavy jacket or coat. The advantage of this system is the ability of several layers to trap and hold the warm body heat. It also gives you the freedom to adjust the amount of clothing needed for the prevailing condition. As discussed elsewhere, wool or pile attire always should be part of your wilderness wear, because those fabrics have the unique ability to keep you warm even when wet. On the other hand, down garments lose their insulating value when penetrated by moisture.

A warm hat is also important cold weather protection, because about one third of the heat your body radiates can be lost through the exposed head. Thus, the old adage "when your feet get cold, put on your hat" holds true; overall body temperature can be maintained better when your head is covered. Avoid tight-fitting clothes and boots that may restrict circulation. In addition to the regular equipment and supplies you have planned for the outing, take extra socks, gloves or mittens, a warm cap, matches in a waterproof container, candles (for warmth as well as light), fire starter, and high-energy food.

Another important consideration in cold weather camping is adequate shelter and insulation. In addition to being water repellent, modern backpacking tents also have the ability to insulate the user from wind, while maintaining a higher temperature by trapping body heat. A ground pad for sleeping also offers the user protection from the cold.

Remaining dry is as important as remaining warm during cold spells, because moisture is one of the major elements that creates hypothermia problems. Thus, proper water-repellent or waterproof clothing should always be a part of your wardrobe. It is, however, important to know that moisture can be created by body perspiration that collects inside a poorly ventilated system of clothing. This is particularly common when wearing a waterproof outer layer. Thus, be aware that internal moisture can cause the same problems as moisture from external sources. In order to guard against the build-up of body moisture in our clothing, it may become necessary to cut down on physical activity during the time the waterproof garment is being worn.

Hot weather creates its own problems for backpackers. The task of remaining cool during hot days is best accomplished by wearing loosely-fitting clothes that can be opened at the collar and waist. A loose-fitting hat can also shade while allowing heat to escape from the head. During extremely hot spells, it may be necessary to restrict travel to the cooler part of the day—during the early morning and early evening hours. When possible, campsites and rest areas should be well shaded. Out of necessity, the daily pace must be slow enough to allow the body to adjust to the prevailing temperature. During such times, we tend to lose large amounts of body fluid, which must be constantly replenished by drinking freely.

Should bad weather include a lightning storm, stay away from exposed places where you will be taller than the immediate surroundings. Remember that wet things tend to conduct electricity, so when possible, stand on objects that are dry and nonconducting. Stay away from tall trees or other tall features and do not stand on wet, marshy soil or in the open. In mountain regions it is very common for thunderstorms to take place in the early afternoons of the summer. As a result of this predictable phenomenon, experienced hikers and climbers will avoid the mountain peaks during that time of day.

With extended periods of bad weather, it is sometimes difficult to maintain high spirits, particularly when confined to a tent for several days upon end. Veteran campers often bring along a good paperback book, a deck of cards, or a miniature chess set to help keep their minds occupied during such times.

Terrain Factors

Different types of terrain can create hazardous situations for the unwary hiker. However, snowfields, streams, talus, and scree fields can all be safely and enjoyably negotiated as long as proper safety precautions are considered.

In the mountain areas of the west, it is common to find large fields of snow remaining well into the summer months. Most snowfields are commonly found on north-facing slopes, which receive very little sun. During the summer, the snowpack constantly cycles through stages of freezing and thawing as the warm afternoons create the thaw, and the cool evenings allow the snow to set up or freeze again. When the snow is hard during the evening and early morning hours, it is easy to traverse, because the hiker does not sink through the crust with each step. In fact, hikers often prefer to travel on this snow rather than on dry land, because the surface is flat and smooth, and a good hiking pace usually can be maintained. On the other hand, travel on snowfields during hot afternoons can create serious problems if the snow or ice has turned soft, causing the hiker to sink up to the knee or waist with each step.

The proper technique for crossing or ascending steep snowfields is to kick footholds into the snow or ice. Each member of the party should use the same footholds and continue to improve upon them by kicking even deeper steps. Also, as a safety precaution, individuals ought to spread out along the route rather than bunch up in one spot on the snowfield. Because a great deal of energy is normally used by the leader to make the initial footholds, it is desirable to have others rotate into the leadership position from time to time.

Descending steep snowfields usually can be accomplished by use of the *plunge step*. This technique involves straightening the leg and, with the full weight of the body behind it, plunging the heel of the boot down on the snow. The impact provides a firm step that is usually quite stable. A rhythm of steps and plunges allows you to descend in quick order. Yet another technique of descending a snowfield is the *glissade* —a ski-like action without the use of skis. The knees are slightly bent, the arms are held out for balance, and the boots are allowed to slip down the snowfield. There are, of course, certain slopes that are too steep to safely use the techniques just described in a safe manner. Crossing such slopes should be avoided altogether, unless you are skilled in the use of an ice axe and climbing ropes.

Another hazard associated with snowfields is the snow avalanche. When traveling in areas containing avalanche dangers, use extreme caution and either be knowledgeable of the hazards, or be accompanied by someone who is. Fortunately, snow avalanche dangers are greatly reduced during the summer months, because thawing tends to settle and stabilize the snow.

The safest routes for travel in avalanche country are on ridgetops and slightly on the windward side, away from cornices. Cornices are caused by snow deposits on the leeward side of peaks and saddles. If you cannot travel on ridges, the next safest route is in the valley as far from the bottom of the slope as possible. Take advantage of areas containing dense timber or rocky outcrops, because they serve as islands of safety.

It is not uncommon during off-trail travel in the mountains to traverse large fields of broken rocks that accumulate at the foot of steep slopes. These heaps of rock are commonly referred to as *talus*. At times, the size of the rocks in talus fields can be quite large, thus requiring careful footing when hopping or jumping from one rock to another. After some practice, the technique of boulder hopping can be fun and relatively safe, as long as the hiking boots used have a good tread. When the rocks are wet there is a need to be particularly careful; even good Vibram soles have been known to slip under such conditions.

Another commonly traveled rock surface is known as *scree*. It is a pile of small or broken stones that also tends to accumulate at the foot of a steep slope. Hikers and climbers commonly take advantage of scree slopes when descending mountains, because the small, broken stones tend to offer a firm footing once they have settled from the initial impact of each step of the foot. Scree tends to slide momentarily downward with each plunge of the foot and, as a result, the hiker can get a quick and exhilarating ride to the bottom of a slope. On occasion, it is easy to allow oneself to be carried away with the speed and end up sliding out of control. One should take time when descending these rocky places.

Large trees that remain standing after they have died can

create a dangerous situation in campgrounds and along hiking trails. These trees have been known to crash to the ground during strong winds. Always establish your camp well away from such hazards.

A final word of precaution should be said about stream crossings. A fall in a fast-running stream can create a real problem, particularly if you are held under the water because of the weight of your backpack. It is for this reason that you should always unbuckle the hip belt to your pack before attempting to cross any body of water. This same practice is also recommended when traversing any narrow ledge or high area. The intent is to be able to get rid of the pack as quickly as possible.

Wildlife

Observing wild animals in their natural environment can add great pleasure to a backpacking experience. Many of us venture into the backcountry in hopes of obtaining a glimpse of creatures that normally do not frequent the urban environment. Too often it is easy to forget that these animals are wild and, as such, are unpredictable in their behavior. For this reason, we should not attempt to entice them with food or try to get close enough to touch or pet them.

Bears can be menacing problems in well-used campsites. This is because they often visit such areas while looking for a free handout. As they are creatures of habit, they will return to any area where food was once found. An area that is frequented by bears is the wrong place to pitch a tent.

One of the best ways to deter bears, and other animals as well, is to select an open and elevated campsite where your presence would be more easily detected, and you would be less likely to surprise the animal. Particularly in grizzly bear country, it is reassuring to locate your shelter near a climbable tree. Also, it is wise to locate your food cache and cooking area well away from your campsite (see Fig. 6.1).

To properly bearproof your camp, establish a general group cooking area and food storage site at least 100 yards downwind from your sleeping area. All food and garbage should be sealed in plastic bags and, if possible, suspended high above the ground. This can be accomplished by attaching a rock to one end of a

Fig. 6.1. In bear country, locate your sleeping area near a climbable tree; locate your cook site and food storage area 100 yards downwind.

nylon rope and throwing the rock over a high tree limb. The other end of the rope is then attached to the food bag and hoisted into the air. Because animals are capable of climbing trees, suspend the food bag three or four feet below the tree and approximately four feet out from the trunk. Bears are capable of reaching high objects, so suspend the bag at least 12 feet above the ground. A more foolproof technique is to suspend the food cache between two trees (see Fig. 6.2). Although this process is more time-consuming and requires a very long rope, it eliminates the possibility of animals reaching the food from a tree limb.

Here are some things you can do to eliminate odors that may attract bears:

1. Avoid cooking smelly or greasy foods.
2. Cook with a stove instead of making a campfire.
3. Use freeze-dried food instead of fresh food.
4. Wash pots and pans immediately following their use.
5. Store all food items in tightly-sealed containers.
6. Don't throw away or bury garbage and food containers.

Fig. 6.2. For protection from bears, resource managers have constructed food caches in some designated backcountry campsites such as this one in Yellowstone National Park.

8.   Dispose of fish entrails by burning completely in a very hot fire. (In grizzly country, puncture the air bladder and drop entrails in deep water where they will decompose naturally.)
9.   Keep sleeping bags and personal gear clean and free of food odor.
10.   Don't sleep in the same clothes you wore while cooking.
11.   Store all odorous products (toothpaste, soap, etc.) as though they were food.
12.   Don't use perfumes, deodorants, and other sweet-smelling substances.

In addition, women may wish to stay out of grizzly bear country during their menstrual period. In general, remember: personal cleanliness is good insurance.

There are no hard and fast rules to ensure protection from a bear attack, but taking all the precautions may reduce the risks. If possible, don't hike alone in bear territory. Stay with the group and watch for signs, such as droppings, tracks, or diggings, that indicate bears are in the area. If you spot a bear, make a wide detour around it and stay as far away as possible. Generally, bears will try to avoid people, so it is a good idea to make your presence known. Many hikers wear bells, dangle a can of rattling pebbles, whistle, talk loudly, clap, or sing in hopes that the noise will prevent a surprise encounter with a bear. Noise, however, is not a foolproof way of avoiding bears.

If you see a bear, give it plenty of room. Do not make abrupt moves and noises that would startle the animal. Slowly detour, keeping upwind so the bear will get your scent and know you are there. If you can't detour, wait until the bruin moves away from your route.

If you approach a bear, it may think you are invading its privacy and react accordingly. Because bears have poor eyesight, they may approach you simply out of curiosity. In such circumstances, it may be effective to speak softly to the animal. By all means, never allow yourself to get between a sow and her cubs. The motherly instinct is to protect the young by attacking.

What should you do if you are suddenly confronted by a bear? Whatever you do, try to remain calm. If the bear is not aggressive and merely stands its ground, you probably should stand still too. Don't run. This may excite the bear into pursuit, particularly if the bear happens to be a grizzly. Grizzlies can attain short bursts of speeds up to 40 miles per hour, so running away is a poor option.

One of the best methods of escaping a bear, especially a grizzly, is to climb a tree. Most adult grizzlies cannot climb trees, and grizzly cubs and black bears often can be discouraged from climbing. As some grizzly bears can stand well over seven feet tall, make sure you climb at least 12 feet up the tree.

If you cannot reach a tree and the bear continues to advance, it may help to drop some sizable item—a bedroll, jacket, or pack—to divert the bear and give you time to retreat. If a black bear actually does attack, the recommended action is to fight it off. Even young children have fought enough to deter potentially fatal black bear injuries. If a grizzly bear charges, your best resort is to assume the "cannonball" position to protect your head and stomach while playing dead. Lie on your stomach or side with legs drawn up to your chest and hands clasped over the back of your neck. Grizzlies have passed by people in this position without harming them. Lying still in this position takes lots of courage—but it may prevent permanent injury or even death.

To avoid putting yourself through such a gruesome experience, you may wish to consider "Counter Assault," a non-lethal spray retardant. This bear repellent is a relatively new product available on the market. For ready access, a quick release clip permits the spray can to be worn on your pack strap or belt. When activated, the nozzle puts out a wide spray, which eliminates the need for accurate aim. Counter Assault contains capsicum, a red-pepper derivative, which repels bears. Research and field tests indicate capsicum emitted from a spray can does, in fact, temporarily immobilize aggressive bears by causing an intense stinging in the eyes, nose, mouth, respiratory tract, and lungs. Thus, capsicum spray could prove an important tool in allowing people and bears to co-exist in the wilderness. Due to limited demand, Counter Assault is relatively hard to find in outdoor retail shops. The spray can be ordered from Bushwacker and Backpack Supply Company, P.O. Box 4721, Missoula, Montana 59806, (406) 728-6241.

The mountain lion is another large animal you should know about. Until recently, there have been relatively few human encounters with these chiefly nocturnal, secretive, and seldom-seen large cats. Within the last few years, however, this has changed. Although incidents are still rare, the number of children and adults injured and even killed by mountain lion attacks has been steadily increasing each year.

In the unlikely event of a mountain lion encounter, what should you do? Although there are no hard and fast rules, wildlife management professionals suggest not turning your back on the animal or attempting to run from it. Likewise, *do not* play dead. What you *should* do is stay calm and slowly back away while facing the animal. Throwing an object at the cat may help to scare it away, as might doing something to enlarge your image, such as holding a pack over your head or opening up your jacket like bird wings. Any young children accompanying you ought to be picked up off the ground.

Although our discussion of wildlife problems has focused on large animals, there is actually a greater likelihood you will have trouble with small animals such as squirrels, chipmunks, mice, skunks, and porcupines. These creatures have been known to eat holes through tents to get at food stored inside. On occasion, they also will devour axe handles and the straps of backpacks because of the salty taste created from human perspiration. Don't neglect these little critters.

Emergency Procedures in the Backcountry

Each year visitors to our backcountry areas face serious injuries, and some die needlessly. They fall victim to a wide assortment of problems because they don't know how to protect themselves from the natural environment. Backpackers need to be prepared to cope with the hazards discussed in this section.

First Aid

The importance of an adequate first-aid kit cannot be stated too strongly. There are, however, few commercial first-aid kits that are suitably designed for emergency situations in the backcountry. The best first-aid kit is one you compile yourself, with the aid of your physician for your personal needs. Universal items can be found at a local drug store, which makes restocking of depleted materials easy. Recommended basic items for a first-aid kit are presented in Appendix F.

Wilderness travel dictates that individuals be responsible for themselves and other members of their party. If injured in the woods, you cannot simply call a doctor; you must rely on your own common sense. Because of this, no first-aid kit can replace first-aid training. A first-aid course dispels misunderstandings about treatment procedures, and provides the facts and knowledge needed to be self-sufficient while away from civilization. Talk to your local chapter of the American Red Cross for information about their courses.

Some fatalities are caused by a failure to identify illness or injury in time and to take appropriate action. Familiarize yourself with the symptoms and treatments for the more common emergency medical problems.

Altitude Sickness

Rapid ascent by persons not used to altitudes over 7,000 feet can result in what is known as altitude or mountain sickness.

Symptoms can include headache, lack of appetite, nausea, vomiting, and insomnia. Even slight physical effort can produce troublesome shortness of breath. Pounding or palpitations of the heart may be noticed. Sleep can be difficult. Respiration may assume the pattern of several very deep, rapid breaths followed by a period of shallow or even absent breathing before deep, rapid breaths begin once again. Most of these problems are due to a lack of oxygen in the body's central nervous system and usually disappear when the victim becomes better adapted to altitude. Most of the symptoms stop within 24 to 48 hours after arrival at altitude, although some shortness of breath, lack of appetite, and headache may persist.

Rest during the first 24 hours at altitude is helpful in preventing altitude sickness. When it does occur, however, the more serious symptoms can often be alleviated by descent to a lower elevation for a day or two. Conscientious effort to consume adequate amounts of food and liquids is also recommended. At least two quarts of liquid should be drunk daily, and four quarts are preferable. Though altitude sickness is extremely disagreeable, it is not life-threatening.

High Altitude Pulmonary Edema

A disorder called High Altitude Pulmonary Edema (HAPE), although apparently rare, is extremely dangerous, because deaths can result within six to 10 hours from the onset of symptoms. HAPE is the presence of excessive fluid in the air sacs (alveoli) of the lung that interferes with the absorption of oxygen by the small blood vessels (capillaries) of the lung.

Although the set of conditions that results in HAPE is very complex and poorly understood, diagnosis is not difficult. A dry, persistent cough and shortness of breath are early signs of problems. Shortness of breath soon becomes very noticeable, as does rapid and noisy respiration. Bubbling sounds may be heard, as if the victim is breathing through liquid—as indeed is the case. The pulse is very rapid (160-180), there is a blue tinge to the skin, and a froth from the mouth appears and turns red as blood is coughed.

Treatment for HAPE should take place at the onset of the earliest symptoms. Immediate and rapid descent can often eliminate the problem and restore normal breathing. If oxygen is available, give it at four liters per minute while descending. Adequate acclimatization seems to be the best protection against HAPE. Above 10,000 feet, at least one day should be allowed for each thousand feet of altitude gained. As with altitude sickness, adequate fluid intake is extremely important.

Hypothermia

The number-one killer of outdoor recreationists is hypothermia—more commonly called exposure. Simply put, this is a loss of body heat at a rate greater than it can be produced, causing a drop in the body's inner-core temperature. Lowering of the internal temperature of the body leads to mental and physical collapse. Although hypothermia is caused by exposure to cold, it is aggravated by moisture, wind, and exhaustion. Hypothermia can occur well above freezing. Deaths have been recorded when the temperature never dropped below 50° F. Many outdoor enthusiasts simply cannot believe such temperatures can be dangerous.

Wet clothes tend to lose their insulating value. Wind can drive cold air under and through wet clothing, creating a refrigeration effect as it evaporates moisture from the surface. This cold affects the individual slowly and subtly, sometimes producing lapses in memory, errors in judgment, clumsiness, and loss of coordination. The victim is unaware that these mental effects are happening.

There are three consecutive stages of hypothermia. First, the body undergoes uncontrollable shivering, which is an attempt to generate heat and maintain a normal body temperature. This stage will last as long as the body has readily available nutrients (sugars and starches). During the second stage, shivering stops because the body no longer has the fuel necessary to produce heat. Cold now reaches the brain, depriving the victim of judgment and reasoning power. The individual will be clumsy, forgetful, and incapable of making the decisions necessary to save his or her life. The third and final stage sees the victim's internal temperature continuing downward until, without immediate treatment, this slide leads to stupor, collapse, and death.

Hypothermia victims will usually deny that they are in

trouble. It is better to believe the symptoms rather than the sufferer. To restore vital body heat, get the victim out of the wind and rain and into the best shelter available. Remove all wet clothes and replace them with dry garments. If fully conscious, the person should be given warm, sweetened liquids. Put the victim into a sleeping bag and have someone else also get into the bag in order to provide body heat. Remember, placing a hypothermia victim in a cold sleeping bag will do no good because he or she cannot produce enough heat to keep the inner-core body temperature at survival level. Skin-to-skin contact is the most effective treatment. If the victim is able to eat, give the person food with high carbohydrates.

In order to prevent hypothermia, dress for warmth, wind, and wetness—the three W's of hypothermia prevention. Remember that clothing loses much of its insulating value when wet, but wool retains more insulation value than any other fabric. Put on rain gear before you get wet; put on wool clothing and wind gear before you begin shivering. Always protect the insulating value of down clothes by keeping them dry. The same holds true with a down sleeping bag. A wet down garment amounts to nothing more than two layers of thin nylon. Also, carry emergency food that is high in energy and eat regularly.

Dehydration

Two quarts of water are required daily by an adult. Four or more quarts are required if one is involved in any kind of strenuous activity, such as backpacking. In order to avoid dehydration, simply drink often—even if you do not feel thirsty. Monitor the volume, frequency, and color of your urine. If you are producing clear urine at least five times a day, you're drinking enough. Cloudy or dark urine, or urinating less than five times a day, means you are running the risk of dehydration. Anyone who loses one and one-half quarts of water without replacing it, will have a 25-percent loss of stamina.

Frostbite

Exposure of inadequately protected flesh to sub-freezing temperatures can cause frostbite. Tissue damage is caused by the reduced blood flow to the extremities. Whenever a person's skin becomes pale or glossy, incipient frostbite should be suspected, and the skin must be covered and warmed. Skin with superficial frostbite is white, waxy, and firm to the touch. In stages of severe frostbite the skin is white and the area is hard throughout. Do not rub the injured tissue because doing so might break the skin. Also, never apply snow or attempt to thaw the area in cold water.

Superficial frostbite can be treated in the field by warming the frozen part in the armpit or against the abdomen of someone else. Try to prevent the spread of frostbite by changing into dry clothing, especially dry mittens and socks.

For severe cases of frostbite, the problem becomes much greater if medical facilities are not close at hand. If a frostbitten foot or leg has not thawed, the patient can walk out to medical care. However, once rewarming has started, the victim is unable to walk and is in extreme pain. Therefore, some situations will dictate the necessity to delay thawing until medical facilities are reached.

Snowblindness

Long exposure of the eyes to snow and sun can cause pain, itching, and defective vision. Snowblindness is the result of sunburn in the eye, which usually goes away if not aggravated. Treatment should involve the use of double-lens goggles or, in severe cases, a blindfold. Prevention is by far the best treatment. Always include a good pair of sunglasses as part of your equipment.

Snakebite

Of the thousands of poisonous snakebites reported each year, very few prove fatal, even when the bites have gone untreated. Many more people die from bee and wasp stings than from snake bites. The seriousness of a bite depends upon such factors as the size and kind of snake, the potency and amount of venom present in the snake at the particular time, the size and physical condition of the victim, and whether or not a venom was injected into or near a vital organ.

When it comes to poisonous snakebites, the key word is "envenomization," which refers to the venom entering your body while the snake bites. It's estimated that 20 percent of the people bitten by rattlesnakes, and 30 percent of those struck by cottonmouth water moccasins and copperheads walk away with no venom within.

If someone is bitten, try to identify the snake or at least determine whether or not it is poisonous. The bite of a nonpoisonous snake appears as two rows of teeth marks and should be treated like any other puncture wound. If the snake is one of the pit vipers, there will be one or two deep fang marks or punctures, although you may not be able to actually see them. If the snake did leave poison, there would likely be instant burning at the bite site followed within an hour by discoloration, swelling, pain, or tingling at the bite. Also, within minutes after an envenomization, a metallic, rubbery, or tingling taste appears in the victim's mouth. After some hours, there will be symptoms of bruising, skin discoloration, blood blisters, chills, fever, muscle spasms, decreased blood pressure, headache, nausea, blurred vision, breathing difficulty, and possibly unconsciousness.

Unnecessary injuries have resulted from improper treatment of snakebite. The most common error is severing blood vessels or tendons when unwisely cutting an x over a bite. The old cross-cut and suction treatment has been determined to be dangerous. The best course of action is a conservative one. Should it be possible to obtain medical aid within an hour, then hurry to get it, for the most helpful treatment is a prompt injection of antivenom to counteract the poison and minimize pain and discomfort. Whether medical assistance is available or not, direct your immediate efforts toward slowing down the spread of the poison and treating the victim for shock. Immobilize the affected limb, and apply a constricting band (bandanna or strip of cloth) directly above and below the bite area. Do not twist the bands with a stick; you are not trying to apply a tourniquet to stop circulation, but are merely attempting to slow it down in order to retard the swelling and the spread of the venom. Then, without cutting the skin, attempt to suck out the poison. Apply a cooling agent to the area to slow down circulation and relieve pain.

Heat Exhaustion

The symptoms of heat exhaustion are moist, clammy skin, dilated pupils, faintness, nausea, palpitations, sweating, and headache. Treat by allowing complete rest in a cool area. Also, fluids by mouth are beneficial.

Heat Stroke

Dry, flushed skin, and very high body temperature indicate a serious problem called heat stroke. Other symptoms include confusion, staggering, headache, and eventually coma. Failure of the perspiration mechanism causes the body temperature to climb to 105-106 degrees. The treatment is to lower the body temperature immediately by application of cold, wet towels or by placing the victim in snow, a cold stream, or a lake until the temperature is near normal.

Blisters

Poorly-fitting boots and temperature extremes are most often the causes of blisters on the feet. This is the most common ailment of backpackers. Neglecting the feet can lead to complete incapacitation in the backcountry. The first signs of blisters are hot spots or sore areas created from the boots rubbing on an area of the foot. Treatment for these early symptoms often prevents further problems. Stop immediately, change to dry socks, and readjust the boot lacings to reduce internal movement and rubbing of the foot.

If a small blister forms, do not open it. Large blisters should be washed with soap and then drained by inserting a sterilized needle under the skin just beyond the edge of the blister. The needle should be sterilized properly by heating in a flame. Do not wipe off the smudge before use. Apply a sterile bandage and treat the blister as an open wound. Use felt tape or moleskin around the blister, not on it, to relieve the pressure and prevent rubbing of the area while walking.

Proper preparation before and during a hike can cut down on foot problems. Clip your toenails close before trip departure. The skin of the foot can also be toughened by swabbing tincture of benzoin on all toes and pressure points. This sticky liquid will take only a few minutes to dry. Then the feet should be dusted with powder.

For those who have chronic blister problems, try covering potential blister areas with moleskin or adhesive tape prior to beginning the hike. Apply tape or moleskin directly over well-dried tincture of benzoin.

Use two pairs of socks; a lighter nylon, poly, or silk one first, then a thicker wool pair. The inner sock will cut down on any rubbing or friction and will allow moisture from perspiration to pass through to the outer sock. Remember to tighten your boot laces for long downhill sections of your hike. Tighter laces will prevent the feet from sliding forward and rubbing on the inside of the boot. When walking downhill, there is a tendency for boot laces to become looser in the lower eyelets and tighter in the upper ones. To keep this from happening, it is helpful to insert a double loop in the shoestring about halfway up the tongue of the boot prior to lacing the upper half. The double loop creates enough friction to prevent the laces from moving.

Illness from Water

There is nothing more delightful to the backpacker than drawing a cold cup of water from a fast-rushing stream or crystal-clear mountain lake. Although there are many places in the backcountry where we can still find pure water, we must always use caution to be sure it is safe for consumption. If there is any question that water may not be potable, disinfect it.

Unfortunately, even in the high mountain regions of most remote wilderness areas, giardiasis has now become a serious problem caused by drinking infected water from streams or lakes. The disease is caused by a microscopic organism, *Giardia lamblia*.

Symptoms usually show up within two weeks and include stomach cramps, diarrhea, bloating, and loss of appetite. Some people show no symptoms, but remain carriers for months or years. Most individuals are unknowingly infected and often return home from their backcountry trip before the onset of symptoms. If you show symptoms within two or three weeks after drinking untreated water, you should suspect giardiasis and so inform your doctor. With proper diagnosis, the disease is curable with prescription medication.

Giardia are carried in the feces of humans and some domestic and wild animals. The cysts of giardia may contaminate surface water supplies such as lakes, streams, and rivers. Contaminated natural waters may be clear, cold, and free-running, and they can look, smell, and taste just fine. Wildlife may be observed drinking without hesitation from these sources. Nonetheless, giardia may still be present. Therefore, for your own protection, all natural waters should be suspected of harboring this organism.

There are several acceptable techniques for disinfecting raw water. The most certain treatment to destroy giardia is to boil water for at least one minute. Common enteric pathogens—microorganisms that cause disease when ingested—die at temperatures as low as 140 degrees Fahrenheit, provided they are cooked long enough. In 160-degree water, giardia dies within a minute, and bacteria and viruses die after a minute at 180 to 190 degrees (1). While giardia is killed at temperatures below boiling, even at high altitudes, heating water to a full boil for one minute avoids the need for a thermometer to measure water temperature. As mentioned, one minute of boiling will destroy other kinds of organisms causing waterborne disease, but at high altitudes you should maintain the boil three to five minutes for an additional margin of safety.

Boiling causes water to taste flat because the air has been removed. You can restore the oxygen and good flavor by vigorously shaking the water container or pouring the water from one container to another several times.

Chemical disinfectants such as iodine or chlorine tablets or drops are not yet considered as reliable as heat in killing giardia, although these products work well against most waterborne bacteria and viruses that cause disease. Until current research better determines the optimal amount of iodine or chlorine required to kill giardia, and the necessary duration of exposure at various water temperatures, these chemicals cannot be recommended for routine disinfection of water. In an emergency where chemical disinfection is necessary, use an iodine-based product because it is more effective than chlorine under certain water conditions. Iodine, either in crystals or tablets, is available from pharmacies and outdoor shops. You can also use iodine from the first-aid kit (two percent tincture of iodine) by adding 20 drops per one gallon of raw water. For quantities of water greater or smaller than one gallon, increase or decrease the dosage proportionately. Iodine can be harmful if directions are not followed carefully. If possible, filter or strain the water first, and then allow the iodine to work at least 30 minutes before drinking. If the water is cold or cloudy, wait at least an hour or use additional iodine.

Filtration is yet an additional way of removing microorganisms from water. Water-purifying filters usually consist of a pump that forces water through a ceramic filter for instant purification. Some light, portable filters available for use in the backcountry can remove objects as small as two to 0.1 microns in diameter (See Fig. 6.3). At a diameter of six to eight microns, a giardia cyst is big by comparison.

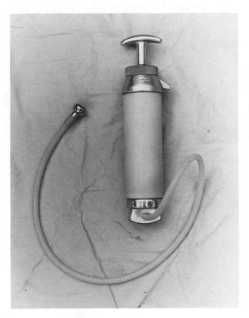

Fig. 6.3. A portable filter, such as this Katadyn model, effectively removes microorganisms from contaminated water.

Be sure your filter removes giardia cysts. Some manufacturers claim their filters do so, but few have actually been tested in unbiased laboratories. Check product literature to ensure that the filter will remove particles as small as one micron in diameter and cannot be easily contaminated by unfiltered water. Granular charcoal filters are not effective in removing giardia, and some filters that do remove giardia may not remove bacterial and viral agents that cause diarrhea. In such cases, you would still need to use chemical disinfectants in the filtered water.

1. "Safe Water On Less Fuel," *Outside*, October 1990, p. 28.

Suggested Reading

Angier, Bradford. 1984. *The Master Backwoodsman*. Fawcett Columbine, 224 pp.

Angier, Bradford, and Zack Taylor. 1983. *Camping on the Go Cookery*. Stackpole, 156 pp.

Antell, Steve. 1980. *Backpacker's Recipe Book*. Pruett Publishing Co., 106 pp.

Arnold, Robert E., M.D. 1973. *What to Do About Bites and Stings of Venomous Animals*. Collier.

Axcell, Claudia, et. al. 1986. *Simple Foods for the Pack*. Sierra Club, 256 pp.

Barker, Harriett. 1981. *The One-Burner Gourmet*. Contempora, 294 pp.

Bevan, Dr. James. 1979. *The Pocket Medical Encyclopedia and First-Aid Guide*. Simon and Schuster, 144 pp.

Blandford, Percy W. 1984. *Maps and Compasses: A User's Handbook*. Tab Books, 243 pp.

Bridge, Raymond. 1981. *America's Backpacking Book*. Scribner's, 390 pp.

Bunnell, Hasse, and the editors of *Backpacker* magazine. 1981. *The Backpacker's Food Book*. Simon and Schuster, 319 pp.

Darvill, Fred T. 1985. *Mountaineering Medicine: a Wilderness Medical Guide*. Wilderness Press, 11th ed. 68 pp.

Ewert, Alan W. 1989. *Outdoor Adventure Pursuits: Foundations, Models, and Theories*. Publishing Horizons, 234 pp.

"Finding Your Way with Map and Compass." 1987. Dept. of the Interior, U.S. Geological Survey, National Cartographic Information Center.

Flemming, June. 1986. *The Well-Fed Backpacker*. Vintage, 3rd ed., 181 pp.

Flemming, June, and Wendy Wallin. 1982. *Staying Found: the Complete Map and Compass Handbook*. Vintage Books, 159 pp.

Fletcher, Colin. 1984. *The New Complete Walker III*. Alfred A. Knopf, 1984, 3rd ed., 668 pp.

Forgey, William, M.D. 1987. *Wilderness Medicine*, 3rd ed., ICS Books, 152 pp.

Gill, Paul G. Jr., M.D. 1991. *Simon and Schuster's Pocket Guide to Wilderness Medicine*. Simon and Schuster, 204 pp.

Glass, Thomas G. Jr., M.D. *Snakebite First Aid*. Available from author, Suite 112, San Antonio, TX 78217, 28 pp.

Greenspan, Rick, and Hal Kahn. 1985. *Backpacking: A Hedonist's Guide*. Moon Publications, 197 pp.

Gunn, Carolyn. 1988. *The Expedition Cookbook*. Chockstone Press, 526 pp.

Hampton, Bruce, and David Cole. 1988. *Soft Paths: How to Enjoy the Wilderness Without Harming It*. Stackpole, 173 pp.

Hart, John. 1984. *Walking Softly in the Wilderness: The Sierra Club Guide to Backpacking*, 2nd ed. Sierra Club Books, 500 pp.

Isaac, Jeff, P.A., and Peter Goth, M.D. 1991. *The Outward Bound Wilderness First-Aid Handbook*. Lyons and Burford, 258 pp.

Jacobson, Cliff. 1989. *The Basic Essentials of Cooking in the Outdoors*. ICS Books, 67 pp.

Jacobson, Cliff. 1988. *The Basic Essentials of Map and Compass*. ICS Books, 66 pp.

Jacobson, Cliff. 1987. *Camping Secrets: A Lexicon of Camping Tips Only the Experts Know*. ICS Books, 161 pp.

Kals, W.S. 1983. *Land Navigation Handbook: The Sierra Club Guide to Map and Compass*. Sierra Club Books, 230 pp.

Kjellstrom, Bkorn. 1976. *Be Expert with Map and Compass*, revised ed. Scribner's, 214 pp.

Manning, Harvey. 1986. *Backpacking One Step at a Time*, 4th ed. Vintage Books, 477 pp.

Martin, Claudine. 1989. *The Trekking Chef*. Lyons & Burford.

McMorris, Bill, and Jo McMorris. 1988. *Camp Cooking: A Backpacker's Pocket Guide*. Lyons & Burford.

McVey, Vicki, and Martha Weston. 1989. *The Sierra Club Wayfinding Book*. Sierra Club Books, 88 pp.

Meyer, Kathleen. 1989. *How to Shit in the Woods*. Ten Speed Press, 77 pp.

Miller, Dorcas. 1980. *The Healthy Trail Food Book*. East Woods Press, 79 pp.

Mitchell, Dick. 1972. *Mountaineering First Aid*. The Mountaineers, 92 pp.

Mooers, Robert L. Jr. 1984. *Finding Your Way in the Outdoors*. Dutton, 275 pp.

NOLS Conservation Practices. 1986. The National Outdoor Leadership School, 10 pp.

Olsen, Larry Dean. 1976. *Outdoor Survival Skills*. BYU Press, 188 pp.

Peters, Ed, Ed. 1982. *Mountaineering: The Freedom of the Hills*, 4th ed. The Mountaineers, 550 pp.

Prater, Yvonne, and Ruth Mendenhall. 1982. *Gorp, Glop & Glue Stew: Favorite Foods from 165 Outdoor Experts*. The Mountaineers, 204 pp.

Randall, Glenn. 1989. *The Outward Bound Map and Compass Handbook*. Lyons & Burford, 112 pp.

Riviere, Bill. 1981. *The L.L. Bean Guide to the Outdoors*. Random House, 299 pp.

Riviere, Bill. 1984. *The Camper's Bible*. Doubleday, 3rd ed., 178 pp.

Roberts, Harry. 1989. *The Basic Essentials of Backpacking*. ICS Books, 64 pp.

Shad, Jerry, ed. 1991. *Wilderness Basics*. Sierra Club, San Diego Chapter, 208 pp.

Shanks, Bernard. 1987. *Wilderness Survival*. Universe Books, 242 pp.

Silva Company. 1989. *Read This, or Get Lost*. Instructional pamphlet.

Silverman, Goldie. 1975. *Backpacking with Babies and Small Children*. Wilderness Press, 122 pp. Sukey, Richard, et. al. 1988. *NOLS Cookery*. National Outdoor Leadership School.

Thomas, Dian. 1985. *Roughing It Easy*, 2nd ed. Warner, 219 pp.

Wilkerson, James A., M.D., Ed. 1986. *Hypothermia, Frostbite and Other Cold Injuries*. The Mountaineers, 105 pp.

Wilkerson, James, A., M.D. Ed. 1985. *Medicine for Mountaineering*. The Mountaineers, 3rd ed., 438 pp.

Winnett, Thomas. 1988. *Backpacking Basics: Enjoying the Mountains With Friends and Family*. Wilderness Press, 3rd ed, 133 pp.

Wood, Robert S. 1982. *The 2 oz. Backpacker*. Ten Speed Press, 2nd ed., 254 pp.

Yaffe, Linda Frederick. 1989. *High Trail Cookery: All-Natural, Home-Dried, Palate-Pleasing Meals for the Backpacker.* Chicago Review Press, 206 pp.

Appendix A

National Scenic Trails

Congressionally-Established Routes	Total Miles
Appalachian Trail	2,110
Pacific Crest Trail	2,600
Continental Divide Trail	3,200
Potomac Heritage Trail	700
North Country Trail	3,200
Natchez Trace Trail	110
Ice Age Trail	1,000
Florida Trail	1,300
Total	**14,220**

National Historic Trails

Congressionally-Established Routes	Total Miles
Lewis and Clark Trail	3,700
Mormon Pioneer Trail	1,300
Oregon Trail	2,170
Iditarod Trail	2,300
Santa Fe Trail	1,200
Nez Perce Trail	1,170
Overmountain Victory Trail	300
Trail of Tears Trail	1,800
Juan Bautista De Anza Trail	1,200
Total	**15,140**

Source: Report on America's National Scenic, National Historic and National Recreation Trails—1989-1990, January 1991, National Park Service, United States Dept. of the Interior,Washington D.C., 25 pp.

Appendix B
Sources of Maps and
Related Information

United States Geological Survey

An index map for any state can be obtained by writing to the USGS. You will receive a map of your chosen state with a grid overlay, each square of the grid bearing the name for the map that is represented. You can also request a small booklet published by the USGS entitled "Topographic Map Symbols." This booklet explains information on map scales and symbols used on maps.

Standard quadrangle maps published in the 7.5-minute series are priced at $2.50 per copy.

Mail orders for topographical maps as well as the requests for a free state index map and the topographic map symbols booklet should be sent to:

USGS Map Sales
Federal Center
Box 25286
Denver, CO 80255
Phone (303) 256-7477

USGS maps can also be purchased over the counter from local commerical outlets. (Check your yellow pages for the USGS catalog for each state.) These maps are also available at USGS offices and state-operated Earth Science Information Centers at the addresses listed below.

Alaska

Room 101, 4230 University Drive
Anchorage, AK 99508-4664

E-146 Federal Building
701 C Street
Anchorage, AK 99513

California

Room 7638, Federal Building
300 North Los Angeles Street
Los Angeles, CA 90012

Room 122, Building 3
345 Middlefield Road
Menlo Park, CA 94025

504 Custom House
555 Battery Street
San Francisco, CA 94111

Colorado

169 Federal Building
1961 Stout Street
Denver, CO 80294

District of Columbia

Room 2650, Interior Building
18th and C Streets NW
Washington, D.C. 20240

Mississippi

Stennis Space Center—NCIC
Building 3101
SSC, MS 39529

Missouri

Mid-Continent Mapping Center—NCIC
1400 Independence Road
Rolla, MO 65401

Utah

Room 8105, Federal Building
125 South State Street
Salt Lake City, UT 84138

Virginia

Room 1C-402, 503 National Center
12201 Sunrise Valley Drive
Reston, VA 22092

Washington

678 U.S. Courthouse
West 920 Riverside Avenue
Spokane, WA 99201

United States Forest Service

National Headquarters

U.S. Forest Service
14th Street and Independence Avenue SW
P.O. Box 96090
Washington, DC 20090
Phone (202) 447-3957

National forest maps and information can be obtained by contacting regional, forest supervisor, or district ranger offices. Regional office addresses are listed below.

Northern Region
Federal Building
P.O. Box 7669
Missoula, MT 59807

Rocky Mountain Region
11177 West Eighth Avenue
P.O. Box 25127
Lakewood, CO 80225

Southwestern Region
Federal Building
517 Gold Avenue SW
Albuquerque, NM 87102

Intermountain Region
Federal Building
324 25th Street
Ogden, UT 84401

Pacific Northwest Region
319 Pine Street SW
P.O. Box 3623
Portland, OR 97208

Pacific Southwest Region
630 Sansome Street
San Francisco, CA 94111

Southern Region
Room 850, 1720 Peachtree Road NW
Atlanta, GA 30367

Eastern Region
Room 500, 310 West Wisconsin Avenue
Milwaukee, WI 53203

Alaska Region
Federal Office Building
709 West Ninth Street
P.O. Box 21628
Juneau, AK 99802

National Park Service

National Headquarters

National Park Service
Public Affairs Office
Interior Building
P.O. Box 37127
Washington, D.C. 20013-7127
Phone (202)208-6843

National park area maps can be obtained at the headquarters office of each park. Addresses of regional offices of the Park Service are:

Alaska Region
2525 Gambell Street
Anchorage, AK 99503-2892

Mid-Atlantic Region
143 South Third Street
Philadelphia, PA 19106

Midwest Region
1709 Jackson Street
Omaha, NE 68102

North Atlantic Region
15 State Street
Boston, MA 02109

Pacific Northwest Region
83 South King Street, Suite 212
Seattle, WA 98104

Rocky Mountain Region
P.O. Box 25287
Denver, CO 80225

Southeast Region
75 Spring Street
Atlanta, GA 30303

Southwest Region
P.O.Box 728
Santa Fe, NM 87501

Western Region
600 Harrison, Suite 600
San Francisco, CA 94107

National Capital Region
1100 Ohio Drive SW
Washington, DC 20242

Bureau of Land Management

National Headquarters

Bureau of Land Management
Public Affairs Office
18th and C Street NW, Room 5600
Washington, DC 20240
Phone (202) 343-5717

The following offices of the Bureau of Land Management can provide maps and information on hiking areas under their jurisdiction:

Alaska State Office
222 West 7th Avenue
P.O. Box 13
Anchorage, AK 99513-7599

Arizona State Office
3707 North 7th Street
P.O. Box 16563
Phoenix, AZ 85011

California State Office
Room E-2841, Federal Office Building
2800 Cottage Way
Sacramento, CA 95825-1889

Colorado State Office
2850 Youngfield Street
Lakewood, CO 80215

Idaho State Office
3280 Americana Terrace
Boise, ID 83706

Montana State Office
222 North 32nd Street
P.O. Box 36800
Billings, MT 59107-6800

Nevada State Office
850 Harvard Way
P.O. Box 12000
Reno, NV 89520

New Mexico (Oklahoma) State Office
U.S. Post Office and Federal Building
P.O. Box 1449
South Federal Place
Santa Fe, NM 87504-1449

Oregon State Office
1300 N.E. 44th Avenue
P.O. Box 2965
Portland, OR 97208

Utah State Office
324 South State Street
Salt Lake City, UT 84111-2303

Wyoming (Nebraska and Kansas) State Office
2515 Warren Avenue
P.O.Box 1828
Cheyenne, WY 82003

Eastern States Office
350 South Pickett Street
Alexandria, VA 22304

(This office handles inquiries for Alabama, Florida, Louisiana, Michigan, Minnesota, Mississippi, Oklahoma, and Wisconsin.)

Canada

Maps of Canada can be obtained from the National Topographical Series by contacting:

Department of Mines and Technical Surveys
Map Distribution Office
615 Boot Sreet
Ottawa, Ontario
Canada

Appendix C
National Wilderness Preservation System

Summary Data

Management Agency	Number of Units	Acreage
U.S. Forest Service	354	32,457,616
National Park Service	43	38,502,565
Fish and Wildlife Service	66	19,332,976
Bureau of Land Management	25	466,949
Total	488*	90,760,106

*Actual units in NWPS: 474—of the 488 units noted above, 14 are managed by more than one agency. Fourteen wilderness areas lie in more than one state—13 areas are in two states, and one area in three.

Number and Total Size of Wilderness Units by State

State	Number of Wilderness Area Units	Number of Acres
Alabama	2	33,396
Alaska	43	56,484,686
Arizona	48	2,037,265
Arkansas	12	128,362
California	54	5,926,158
Colorado	28	2,644,864
Florida	17	1,420,420
Georgia	12	460,215
Hawaii	2	142,370
Idaho	6	4,001,535

State	Number of Wilderness Area Units	Number of Acres
Illinois	1	4,050
Indiana	1	12,935
Kentucky	2	18,056
Louisiana	3	17,046
Maine	1	7,386
Massachusetts	1	2,420
Michigan	14	248,724
Minnesota	3	804,489
Mississippi	3	7,300
Missouri	7	70,860
Montana	15	3,436,578
Nebraska	2	12,375
Nevada	1	64,667
New Hampshire	4	102,932
New Jersey	2	10,341
New Mexico	24	1,609,797
New York	1	1,363
North Carolina	12	109,003
North Dakota	3	39,652
Ohio	1	77
Oklahoma	3	22,524
Oregon	38	2,093,888
Pennsylvania	2	9,705
South Carolina	7	60,539
South Dakota	2	74,074
Tennessee	11	66,714
Texas	6	81,196
Utah	15	802,189
Vermont	6	58,539
Virginia	16	169,453
Washington	30	4,252,344
West Virginia	6	80,361
Wisconsin	6	43,988
Wyoming	15	3,084,640

(Source: *The National Wilderness Preservation System 1964-1989* brochure, The Wilderness Society, 1989.)

Appendix D
Suggested Equipment and Clothing List

This list contains items that may be needed for your outing. Some items may be omitted, depending upon the special conditions of the hiking trip. Refer to Chapter 2 for detailed descriptions of clothing and equipment.

Equipment

Backpack
Backpack rain cover
Day pack
Tent or tarp
Groundcloth
Sleeping bag
Stuff sack
Ground pad or mattress
Stove
Fuel container or cartridge
Pot with lid
Grill
Cup
Bowl
Spoon
Fry pan
Pocket knife
Water container
Water filter
Map
Compass
Sunglasses
First-aid kit (see Appendix F)
Flashlight with extra batteries and bulb
Candle
Waterproof matches in container
1/8" nylon cord (at least 50 feet)
Repair kit: Needle and thread; rip-stop tape; assorted cotter
    pins; wire; pliers; two coins

Toilet items: washcloth, biodegradable soap, toothbrush, toothpaste, dental floss, comb, toilet tissue, hand mirror, chapstick, sun lotion, insect repellent

Clothing

Boots
Camp shoes
Bandanna
Underwear
Belt
Long pants
Walking shorts
Long-sleeved shirt
Short-sleeved shirt
Turtleneck
Jacket
Parka
Poncho
Rain chaps
Hat or cap
Socks
Long underwear
Mittens
Gaiters
Mosquito head net

Hobby equipment

Camera and film
Fishing gear
Fishing license
Pencil stub and notebook
Field books
Binoculars
Fire permit
Camping permit

Food

See Appendix E for a detailed list of suggested food for consideration.

Appendix E
Suggested Menu Items

Following is a list of various foods that can be considered as alternatives for your meal planning. Some items are available at outdoor retail shops, while others can be obtained from your local supermarket or health food store. Most are of the instant, dehydrated, or freeze-dried type.

Breakfast Items
Instant oatmeal
Granola-type cereal
Powdered eggs
Instant pancakes
Powdered maple syrup
Powdered margarine
Dried fruit
Instant rice and raisins

Lunch Items
Freeze-dried salad spreads and mixes (tuna, egg, chicken, ham)
Peanut butter (in plastic bottle)
Beef jerky
Hard and powdered cheeses
Dry salami
Bread sticks, hard crackers, or soft tortillas
Nuts
Dried fruits
Instant hummus spread
Gorp (mixture of peanuts, raisins, mixed nuts, dried fruits, etc.)

Supper Items
Instant and dehydrated soups
Freeze-dried and dehydrated vegetables (green beans, carrots, corn, tomatoes, potatoes, etc.)
Freeze-dried and dehydrated fruits (apples, apricots, bananas, figs, peaches, prunes, raisins, strawberries, etc.)

Freeze-dried dinners (beef stew, chicken stew, chicken almondine, spaghetti and sauce, chili and beans, macaroni and cheese, vegetable stew, turkey tetrazzini, beef stroganoff, potato and beef patties, etc.)
Instant tofu burgers
Instant rice or pilaf, mashed potatoes, couscous, and refried beans
Tacos or enchiladas
Pemmican
Instant ramens
Instant sauce mixes(salsa, enchilada, taco, sour cream, gravy, spaghetti, nacho cheese, etc.)
Desserts (stewed dried fruits with instant dumpling mix, gelatins, popcorn, instant puddings, fruit leather, etc.)

General Considerations
Powdered fruit drink mixes
Instant hot chocolate, coffee, Ovaltine, or tea
Powdered milk
Herbs and spices (Choose a few favorites, such as salt, pepper, oregano, rosemary, cloves, anise, sage, thyme, cinnamon, ground cumin, bay leaves, and dried dill.)

Appendix F
Recommended First-Aid Kit

Tape: two-inch roll
Adhesive compresses: one, two, and four inch sizes
Triangular bandage: cut on bias from 40" cloth
Elastic support bandage: for sprains and strains
Band-aids: four to six, assorted sizes
Moleskin: one roll (for blisters)
Gauze pad: four three by three inch size
Vaseline: for abrasions
Burn ointment or spray
Eye ointment: for pain from snowblindness or eye strain
Ammonia inhalants: three tubes
Antibacterial soap, small bar
Aspirin: six to 12 tablets
Alcohol swabs: four or five
Insect repellent
Kaopectate: small bottle
Antacid: six tablets
Antihistamine: six tablets (for stings, insect bites, colds, hay
    fever, or hives)
Gauze roll: two-inch size
Safety pins, needle, razor blade, and small pair of scissors
Physician's prescriptions, antibiotics, and pain relief medications

Index